From Science to Business

Also by Georges Haour and published by Palgrave Macmillan

RESOLVING THE INNOVATION PARADOX:
Enhancing Growth in Technology Companies

From Science to Business

How Firms Create Value by Partnering with Universities

Georges Haour

Professor, International Institute for Management Development (IMD), Lausanne, Switzerland

&

Laurent Miéville

Former President, Association of European Science and Technology Transfer Professionals, and Director of Technology Transfer, University of Geneva, Switzerland

The authors have asserted their rights to be identified as the authors of this work in accordance with the Copyright, Designs and Patents Act 1988.

First published 2011 by
PALGRAVE MACMILLAN

Palgrave Macmillan in the UK is an imprint of Macmillan Publishers Limited, registered in England, company number 785998, of Houndmills, Basingstoke, Hampshire RG21 6XS.

Palgrave Macmillan in the US is a division of St Martin's Press LLC, 175 Fifth Avenue, New York, NY 10010.

Palgrave Macmillan is the global academic imprint of the above companies and has companies and representatives throughout the world.

Palgrave® and Macmillan® are registered trademarks in the United States, the United Kingdom, Europe and other countries.

ISBN 978–0–230–23651–6

This book is printed on paper suitable for recycling and made from fully managed and sustained forest sources. Logging, pulping and manufacturing processes are expected to conform to the environmental regulations of the country of origin.

A catalogue record for this book is available from the British Library.

A catalog record for this book is available from the Library of Congress.

10 9 8 7 6 5 4 3 2 1
20 19 18 17 16 15 14 13 12 11

Printed and bound in Great Britain by
MPG Group, Bodmin and Kings Lynn

To the young generation

Contents

LIST OF FIGURES

This book is born out of our common passion for effective ways of stimulating job- and wealth-creation through firms effectively leveraging innovations. To be successful in this, the need for firms to incorporate external inputs, if not at all new, will become more acute in the future.

In this work, we look at one type of partner for the firm: universities. In this sense, this follows on from a previous book by one of the authors: *Resolving the Innovation Paradox* describes the novel concept of *distributed innovation*. In this market-oriented, entrepreneurial approach, the firm orchestrates the innovation process, assembling external inputs to complement its own capabilities, in order to develop more effective offerings.

The world must extensively innovate, in an attempt to solve a number of crises – energy, food, water, climate – and to produce more sustainable goods and services, thus embracing novel concepts and approaches. Another central element in today's world is the emergence of China and India as markets and competitors, but also as sources of innovations for the world.

As we face such deep structural transformations, universities and firms must make their full positive contribution to generate jobs and new activities. We thus need more effective partnerships between firms and universities and public laboratories, fully including partners in Asia.

Our complementary professional trajectories bring together the perspectives of firms and universities. This has helped us define what works best in practicing the various modes of knowledge and technology transfer: collaborative research, licensing, and spinning out companies. We also point to future trends in this area. Appropriately, we are based in a country where firm–university partnerships work better than in most countries.

We would like to thank very much numerous colleagues, who have been so generous with their time. Our conversations with them constitute essential contributions. Thanks are also due to our organizations for their support, the University of Geneva and the International Institute for Management Development (IMD).

Geneva   GEORGES HAOUR
LAURENT MIÉVILLE

CHAPTER 1

Firms engage with universities in many different ways

In the so-called 'knowledge economy', two actors, the enterprises and the universities, seem to be destined to work more and more closely. These constitute actors of the Distributed Innovation system, described in a previous book, *Resolving the Innovation Paradox*, by one of the authors. In this novel approach, the innovative company federates various elements from external actors, integrating them with internal capabilities, in order to develop market-oriented, 'high-impact offerings' in an entrepreneurial perspective. In this way, on occasion, the company orchestrates multi-actor innovation projects without being constrained by its own internal capabilities.[1]

Most countries are engaged in sustained attempts at formulating and implementing policies which aim at reinforcing these linkages, sometimes described, not very helpfully, as 'crowdsourcing'. This denotes an effort to federate many individual and institutional inputs. Among these many interactions, the specific and important area of transferring novel knowledge and technology from universities to firms constitutes the subject of this book. This transfer is not a straightforward affair. The path from science to business is fraught with pitfalls. This path involves two very different partners, which have different missions and histories. After a brief introduction on each of these two actors, the different ways of partnering will be reviewed, thus outlining the structure of the book, which concentrates on the three main vehicles for such technology transfer: collaborative research, licensing and spin-out ventures.

Universities and firms, two key actors of the so-called 'knowledge economy'

Universities and firms belong to different worlds. In this chapter, we take a rapid look at some historical aspects of these two actors to underscore their differences in perspective.

Universities

The institutions of universities have been established for many centuries. In China, Nanjing University, founded in 258, was, with more than 10,000 students, the world's largest institution for higher education in the 15th century. In Europe, universities appeared in 1088 in Bologna, and about 1150 in Paris (La Sorbonne) and Oxford. In Bologna, groups of students organized themselves together and contracted with professors as a means of obtaining the license to teach, the *licencia docendi*. This 'bottom-up' process was thus actually regulated by the state.

Europe's universities were heirs of the Greek academies and were a secular response to the scholarly traditions of monasteries. Later, many university campuses indeed incorporated the reflective quadrangles of meditation-prone cloisters, which were themselves derived from Greek and Roman architecture. In the late 18th century, Alexander von Humboldt defined the role of the university as providing a foundation (*Bildung*) to the individual, stating that, in contrast to the relationship in high school, in higher education, 'both the teacher and the student are partners in scholarship'.

Like artists, scientists have long entertained relationships with the leaders of their time, as precursors of technology transfer, while military preoccupations were often the rationale at work. When Archimedes, born in 287BC, who lived his 75 years in Syracuse, was asked by the king Hiero II to detect whether his crown was pure gold, the mathematician and inventor came up with his law on buoyancy. At the time, he was employed as a tutor for the son of the king.

Firms

Corporations are much younger than universities. Roughly, they appeared in the 17th century in Japan (the first being Sumitomo, to exploit copper mines) and France (with Saint Gobain, to produce flat glass and mirrors for the Versailles Palace). Below is a contemporary quote on the duties of the plant manager, from the 'Rules for the Royal Manufacture of Saint Gobain':

> He shall devote all his ability and application to manufacture good glazing and avoid defects which are but too frequent. He shall listen to all ideas on that matter whoever they are coming from. He shall make mature reflections and take the benefit of it, if he finds them good. He shall beware of falling into the mistake of some of his predecessors who, by fantasy and presumption, imagined that all which did not come from them could not be good.

This text, dated December 10, 1728, is remarkable in that, almost three centuries ago, its statement singles out the key concerns of today's management, such as quality and low reject rate, Not Invented Here (NIH) syndrome, the necessity to have an open mind and willingness to listen to suggestions.

One of the pioneering books on management was written by the Frenchman Henri Fayol (1845–1925). In his book *Administration Industrielle Générale*, published in 1916, Fayol, long-time director of the Commentry coal mine, identifies six areas in the firm: technical, managerial, financial, safety, accounting and administration. The role of the manager is to: anticipate, organize, command, coordinate and control. For a long time, management jargon has used military terminology, such as 'attacking a market', 'dominating the competition', 'mobilizing people', to the point of using the old Chinese book of the *Art of War* as a management textbook. More recent managerial jargon distances itself somewhat from the military verbiage, favoring biological metaphors instead: we hear *ad nauseam* phrases such as: 'the DNA of a corporation'.

An important contemporary issue for firms is dealing with the breakneck rate of change they need to take on board to remain competitive. As for tomorrow, the common wisdom is that it will continue to be a 'hyper-competitive' business world, in which 'the only sure thing in the future is *change*'. With the world facing a multiplicity of crises – climate, energy, food and water – which constitute opportunities for entrepreneurs and corporations, change is certainly the operative word for the coming decade(s). This is to be added to the fast-moving, tumultuous nature of the commercial world, where world-wide competitors and the use of information technology continue to brutally disrupt the competitive scene and ways to do business.

Broadly, firms may be subdivided into three categories: corporations, small and medium-size enterprises (SMEs) (below 250 employees), and start-up companies. In an economy, they interact and trade with each other, as part of what is often called an 'ecosystem', to produce goods and services. For example, corporations are usually clients of start-ups in business-to-business transactions. It is therefore desirable that the large companies are not too conservative and are amenable to trying the new offerings of young or much smaller companies.

Connecting the two worlds of firms and universities became even more necessary when different disciplines of science and technology developed their substantial body of knowledge. In the 19th century, a specific point of contact emerged with the research and development (R&D) department. 'Invented' in Germany for improving processes in the chemical industry, the R&D department was staffed by university graduates. For the first time, a systematic process was at work to transfer technology from universities to firms.

Key is not how much firms invest in R&D but how they perform it

One difficult issue with R&D investments is that it is extremely difficult to assess their impact. R&D is only one element of the innovation process, which indeed involves practically the whole firm. Also, what counts is the output success in the marketplace, rather than inputs – the R&D budget. A study by Booz Allen Hamilton, their Global Innovation report (2005), confirms that lavish R&D budgets indeed do not guarantee good performance, measured by commercial success, profitability and market share. It is more critical to leverage astutely the various external sources which can fuel the firm's innovation process, as proposed by the complementary approaches of open and distributed innovation.

Among these external sources, universities and public research laboratories (PROs) seem to be partners of choice for industry.

Firms acquire a competitive advantage through such partnerships. Among the reasons cited by firms, the *Lambert Review*[2] lists the main benefits for firms to work with universities:

- Access to new ideas, breakthroughs
- Access to a large intellectual pool of competencies or technologies
- Leveraging the research budget with public funding schemes
- Spotting and recruiting the brightest young talents
- Expanding pre-competitive research
- Access to specialized consultancy

The same study points to a good correlation between business success and economic performance and university collaboration.[3]

From the OECD *Science, Technology and Industry Outlook 2008*, it is noted that, as a percentage of GDP, tertiary education institutions perform only 0.25 per cent of the R&D carried out in OECD countries. This level has been fairly stable over the last ten years. The percentage is 0.4 for public research organizations. In absolute terms, however, investing in R&D in the higher education sector has experienced a fairly strong growth in recent years, especially in China and Ireland (13 per cent between 2001 and 2006). During that period, the corresponding annual growth in the OECD area has been 3.3 per cent, as compared with 2.8 per cent in the 27 countries of the European Union. These average growth rates point to a global increase of emphasis in partnering with universities and public laboratories.

The USA is often given as an example of a country where the bulk of the world's innovation and growth in two crucial areas, ICTs and life sciences takes place. In a recent book, the former CEO of Amgen, Gordon Binder, gives a perspective on this prowess.[4] In his mind, the key is that the USA has the research capacity, helped by government funding and policy, and, more importantly, the enterprising spirit. This explains why the USA pretty much dominates the market in personal computers and software, semiconductors and biotech drugs.

Ways in which firms and universities engage with each other

There is a wide spectrum of ways in which these two 'partners' interact, directly or indirectly. They flow from the mission of universities, which is excellence in education and in research. These ways are listed below:

(a) *Education*
- firms hire graduates from universities. This is indeed a most powerful way to transfer knowledge and technology
- students carry out graduate work in connection with a firm
- students do internships in firms
(b) *Professional contacts*
- informal contacts between employees of firms and personnel from universities.
- meetings on occasions such as conferences or forums
- professors act as consultants or advisors to firms
(c) *Research*
- contract and collaborative research, either on a one-to-one basis, or as a consortium of firms joining forces to solve a specific issue
- joint laboratories
- donations for long-term relationships, such as endowments for research or professorial chairs
(d) *Vehicles for technology transfer of the outcome of university research*
- selling licenses based on patents owned by the university
- spinning out companies relying on knowledge and patents generated by the university

This wide array of interactions, according to which firms and universities may collaborate and influence each other for positive change in creating new business activity, is illustrated in Figure 1. The methods of engagement are organized by increased institutional character in each of the four categories of interactions and will be discussed in the following sections.

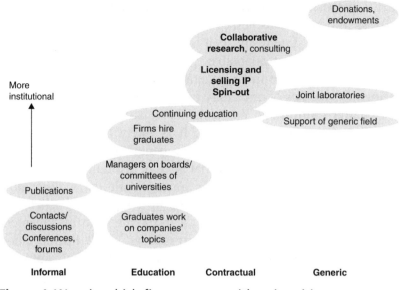

Figure 1 Ways in which firms engage with universities

The graduates are key agents for transferring knowledge and technology

A powerful link between institutions of higher education and firms is indeed constituted by graduates working in companies. This makes it possible to maintain a flow of knowledge and technology moving from university to firm. As an example, Kamil Quadir, following his graduation from an American university, founded the company CellBazaar, to make cell phones available to the population of Bangladesh, where he grew up. In a country where the lack of electricity makes it impossible to have access to internet, millions of individuals are users of CellBazaar for connecting, trading and entertainment.

These alumni can constitute quite a strong 'lobby' to influence the university. We can see this role being played in practice particularly in the USA, but also in the so-called French 'Grandes Écoles', institutions of higher education, which recruit on the basis of competitive exams, two years after the end of high school. In such Institutions, the alumni associations generally have a powerful voice. They may also provide useful networks, helping to develop businesses or finding the next job. This said, beyond general statements such as 'we need more computer scientists' or 'we want adaptable, problem-solvers, effective team players', managers of firms generally cannot, or do not want to, define the specifics of university curricula.

Updating university curricula is relatively straightforward within each scientific discipline. It is likely that there will be agreement on having more and more genetic engineering in life-science studies, for example. What is more difficult is to deal with the balance of disciplines within an academic curriculum: how much mathematics should be taught in a four-year bachelor of science degree, or how much of an introduction to management should engineers receive at undergraduate level? Furthermore, what about an effective education in languages, 'other' cultures, or history and philosophy?

For universities, a difficult adaptation is in the pedagogy. If a medical school wants to introduce the case study method, pioneered by law schools and later used extensively in business schools, a broad agreement has to be found across the various fiefdoms constituted within the medical departments; and additional resources must be found to provide a more hands-on education. A similar issue concerns the use of distance learning. Pioneered in Great Britain, a new institution, the Open University, was created in 1969 in order to facilitate further/ higher education via electronic media – television at the time.

Universities have the 'academic' tradition of individual faculty members pursuing their own specific topics. A true cross-disciplinary approach, which is required to address real-life issues, encounters multiple obstacles in such an environment. Again, because of this fiercely individual orientation – some people would talk about the silo mentality – universities do not do a good job of 'knowledge management'.

A broader debate is whether research constitutes a natural companion activity and nourishing complement to the educational mission of universities. The so-called 'leading institutions' all have strong research activities and, for them, their clear mission is, indeed, excellence in teaching and excellence in research. Some outstanding learning takes place in institutions where the faculties do not carry out research activities however, for example, in a number of small, private universities, or state colleges in the USA. In science and technology fields, how truly pertinent is the slogan 'education through research'?

How universities anticipate the 'needs' of society, so that they best equip their students for the future, is a vast topic, largely influenced by the governance of the universities, as well as the culture and traditions of the country where they operate. Let us only remark that, all over our interdependent world, countries are generally dissatisfied with their own educational system and are trying reforms and adaptations of their institutions, which have been inherited from centuries of tradition.

Universities must indeed work with pupils coming out of high schools. Countries should be much more attentive in making sure that secondary education offers a solid foundation, at a time when, in most parts of the world, a weakening of the general level of pupils is being observed. According to OECD rankings, Finland comes out as providing the best scientific education (particularly in mathematics). Without arguing how valid such rankings are, whether produced by the Programme for International Student Assessment (PISA) or otherwise, it does seem that, by and large, a great strength of Europe, as well as of Asian countries, is precisely that it provides a generally decent level secondary education, a basis for apprehending the world and a foundation on which to build. In Europe, the first recognition of this mission was by Calvin, who created the first secular mandatory secondary school in 1549, in Geneva.

An excessively 'utilitarian' approach of secondary education is counterproductive. In western countries, learning 'dead languages', such as Latin and ancient Greek, goes well beyond learning about language roots; it provides the ability to learn how to learn and to have different 'points of view' on the universe, which is crucial to detect patterns with an open mind, in our interdependent and fast-changing world. In a similar vein, the recent 'utilitarian' decision of China to impose English as a language in high school seems to make sense, but should not be allowed to erode the richness and diversity of the Chinese world. There is hope for this approach, as India does not seem to have lost too much of its extraordinary cultural diversity even after having practiced its own brand of English for many years.

Conversely, people of English mother tongue feel that, because they speak the world language – until Mandarin takes over – they do not need to learn another tongue. As a result, they are severely handicapped in their inability to adopt another point of view, which another language richly provides. In the days when Greek was the 'world language', Herodotus was violently critical of the ethno-centric attitudes of his fellow Greeks towards the barbarians – the non-Greeks…

University–industry consortiums for graduate/ continuing education

Knowledge transfer may be achieved by having industry and university working together to launch a new course. This may be a technical course for continuing education in microelectronics or security of information technology systems, for example. This can also be achieved at the level of post-graduate courses. One example is the master's degree in pharmaceutical medicine for effective drug development, launched in late 2009 under the Innovative Medicines Initiative (IMI). The initiative is funded (€15 million for five years) by the European Union and industry on a 50/50 basis. The consortium is constituted by six universities and 15 companies. The aim is to provide a comprehensive course providing a fully integrated understanding of the complete drug development process, from molecule discovery to market introduction. It is a response to the fact that pharmaceutical companies worldwide have insufficient drug-development pipelines. In recent years, the European Medicine Agency (EMEA) has approved only 20 new drug applications per year. This university–industry initiative aims at making the pharmaceutical innovation process more effective.

Broad linkage between business and universities

At the institutional level, universities have been under increasing pressure to establish connections with the key actor in our economy: companies, small or large. It may be argued that the venerable universities of Cambridge and Oxford did not create business schools to further enhance their academic credibility, but to establish a bridge with the business world. With this in mind, individuals gave each university large donations to establish such bodies: the Judge Institute at Cambridge and the Said Business School at Oxford. A precursor for this situation can be seen when Alfred Sloan, long-time president of the now infamous General Motors, asked the Massachusetts Institute of Technology (MIT) to start a business school in 1952.

Beyond the fact that it makes eminent sense to diligently maintain a rich dialogue with their alumni now employed by firms, universities can secure helpful intelligence on the evolving needs of the enterprises by keeping in contact with the workforce. Universities are increasingly realizing that their alumni represent one of their crucial assets, but few of them dedicate adequate resources, in persons and money, to effectively utilizing this situation.

In 2008, the University of Tokyo launched a new high-level education program for senior executives, most of them alumni, thus reinforcing their connection with the alma mater. The alumni population of the establishment represents privileged access to firms and is, indeed, a great source of professional contacts, as discussed below.

Professional contacts

Through informal contacts between faculties, students or alumni and employees of companies, universities have a position of influence. These contacts are channelled through specific meetings, at conferences and trade shows. Few companies proactively seek out such inputs: by and large, such conversations are opportunistic. This is not to say that they are not influential. Managers indicate that insights and new ideas (up to a third of ideas, in fact) germinate in the course of conversations with 'academics'. Others confirm that, among their key sources of intelligence on technology and markets, a number of selected professors are regularly consulted. One way to make this happen is to participate in conferences and meetings. Another way is to tap into 'expert groups' via the internet. The value of these is uneven, may be because electronic networking is still a recent practice. Occasionally, such informal 'electronic' contacts may lead to a more formal connection covered by a consultancy agreement.

Consultancy agreements occasionally bind an individual professor with a firm. Universities have rules on the terms of the contract, as well as on how many days of consultancy are allowed per year. Increasingly, the university takes an overhead percentage (10–15 per cent) of the consultancy fees, since, after all, professors obtain consultant jobs largely as a result of their affiliation with the institution. Other universities, Imperial College in London for example, channel the consultancy activity of their faculties through a consultancy subsidiary. Other scenarios include consultancy services being lumped together with the technology transfer services, providing collaborative laboratory-based research projects.

The main vehicles by which universities transfer their knowledge and technology to firms constitute the focus of this book, as described below. As an introduction to presenting the structure, *The Triumph of Technology*[5] stresses that the principal challenge for any research organization is to be effective in technology transfer. This is particularly the case for universities.

Focus of this book: collaborative research, licensing and spinning out start-ups

This book focuses on the vehicles for transferring university's knowledge and research results into firms and new businesses. These are: collaborative research, licensing and selling intellectual property (IP) and creating spin-out companies based on university research. These are discussed in turn in the three following chapters.

Chapter 2 describes collaborative research, by which the firm taps into the technical expertise of an external partner – the university or a public laboratory, in this case. It covers a range of possibilities, in terms of the scope of the project – exploring an area or carrying out a focused project – and in terms of the duration – short and highly specific or long-term collaboration of a more generic nature. In all cases, the collaboration must follow a period of discussion and negotiation, allowing the parties to align their objectives.

Chapter 3 discusses another route for transferring technology from university R&D to a firm: it involves selling a license based on a university patent, or selling its intellectual property (IP) outright. Indeed, similar licensing transactions take place between a firm and another firm. Licensing requires specific areas of expertise. By exploiting the patent, the firm improves its business position or builds new activities.

Chapter 4 concentrates on the most complex way of transferring university research and developement (R&D) into a commercial venture. It involves creating a firm, a *spin-off* or *spin-out* start-up company – based on the technology-intensive business idea generated by the university. This process requires considerable know how, in order to bridge the gap separating the novel technical idea from its successful commercial deployment in the market. The start-up may either grow on its own, or be purchased by a corporation, to reinforce its activities. The latter is particularly practiced by the pharmaceutical/biotech sector.

Chapter 5 looks into the particular situation of small and medium-size enterprises (SMEs), as they tap into the knowledge base of universities and public research laboratories. By partnering with external actors, they enhance their innovation-led growth, but encounter specific issues, as the capacities in manpower and finances available in SMEs are more constrained than is the case for corporations. As a result, specific mechanisms must be put in place.

Chapter 6 looks at some specific, critical framework conditions allowing firms to successfully engage with universities, in order to contribute to their business creation process. A comparison between the USA and Europe shows many parallels, whereas Asia is rapidly moving forward. At the country level, the example of Switzerland is described, as it is recognised as handling knowledge and technology most effectively.

Chapter 7 outlines the way forward in the academia–firms partnerships. It points to trends which will impact such partnerships and emerging models of firm–university interactions for generating new business. It details the changes, which both the universities and companies are expected to undergo in the future. On occasion, implications for public policy are underscored.

In the course of the following chapters, two topics are woven into the arguments: sustainable development and Asia. These are discussed below.

The two themes running through this book

Two themes run throughout the following chapters. We believe that they will strongly impact partnerships between firms and universities and public research laboratories, aimed at enhancing activities or creating a new businesses. First, the world needs to go through a metamorphosis in order to become more sustainable. Second, in Asia, in addition to the technological powerhouse of Japan, two countries, China and India, are rapidly evolving and will profoundly affect the world's geography of innovation. These themes are briefly discussed below.

Towards a more sustainable system

In addition to the crisis within the system, triggered by the financial debacle of the Wall Street 'subprime' loans, our world faces a multiplicity of long-term crises: climate change, energy, food, water, raw materials, demographics. These bring opportunities, but also tremendous challenges, whose responses must fully involve firms effectively partnering with universities.

We urgently need positive change towards a more sustainable system. This involves new sources and better management of energy, more responsible operations of the firms, but also inspiring, responsible behaviour on the part of customers. The latter often underestimate the power they have to effect positive change in the world. The need is for a massive amount of innovation to transform our system, while individuals will have to change their lifestyles considerably.

In this transformational process, universities must play their full role, by teaming up with private firms and public institutions. This may be a key element of the constant effort of universities to be ever more 'relevant' to society. The logic is at work in industrialized countries. Academics eagerly cluster around money without, hopefully, losing their soul in the process. Partly as a result of the need to understand better the business world and, possibly, to adopt some of its management practices, senior managers from industrial companies or consultant firms are increasingly selected to become presidents or rectors of universities. Such 'grafts', however, have been often rejected by academic bodies.

This attempt to address 'relevance' concerns the education of students, as well as R&D activities. Although many examples in this book are in the field of science and technology, universities have a lot to offer to firms in non-technical fields, such as social sciences and conceptual innovation.

Asia: fast-growing source of innovations for the world

For the first time in human history, very large, dynamic economies are fast appearing as main actors in on the world stage: China, India and Brazil. As a country, to which so many superlatives could be applied, China is rapidly becoming a world actor in yet another area: *innovation*, in the technical arena, as well as in the business and management sphere. The speed and robustness with which these evolutions take place are the object of some debate, but it is difficult to overestimate the importance of the *China phenomenon* for western economies and firms. In a recent speech, 'The Rise of Asia's Universities',[6] the President of Yale expressed his view that the rise of Asia's universities is a manifestation of globalization. Nations of Asia have increasing access to the resources needed to create institutions of excellence. In conclusion, he salutes this as a very positive trend for the world.

The tremendous dynamism of China's markets

Today's China represents 8 per cent of the world output, as compared with 1 per cent 30 years ago. But it may be more appropriate to speak about the re-emergence of China, since in the 18th century, it is estimated that China accounted for close to 20 per cent of world output.

The sheer size and the growth rate of China, unprecedented in history, results in this: what China sells, such as toys or consumer electronics goods, depresses world prices, while what China buys increases world prices, namely oil and commodities. On the educational side, every year, a number of students close to the population of Paris walks out of Chinese universities with a bachelor degree.

In the stores of Chinese cities, consumer goods are being replaced at an amazing speed. Products, packaging, marketing and branding are the object of extremely rapid changes, in order to satisfy discriminating and fast-changing consumers' demands.

In the 1980s, Japan was the benchmark of a market characterized with a short 'shelf-time' of products and utmost quality. For this reason, non-Japanese companies saw that country as a demanding testing ground, where much could be learned, thus to become more competitive in the world's markets. In many ways, China is currently a test-country in its own right, but this phenomenon is amplified and accelerated by the sheer size, the fast growth and the entrepreneurial spirit of the country. Observers from outside China are somewhat mesmerized by the unusual combination of a very strong command regime and great 'plasticity', which makes it possible to accept a high rate of change.

Innovation goes East

China's relentless efforts in R&D investment are reflected in the (very crude) indicator of patent filings. In 2007, this number increased by 38 per cent over the previous year. China now ranks seventh in the world. This is an indicator of China's fast-increasing investments in this field. This figure now represents 1.5 per cent of GDP, not too far from the 2.3 per cent average figure of the 27 current member states of the European Union. The target is 2.5 per cent of GDP in 2020. Again, these are input figures; they are far from telling the whole story. The country's effort, however, is very substantial and, by design, most Chinese top government officials have an advanced scientific degree, so that they well understand the power of technical innovation for job- and wealth-creation.

In our interdependent world, technology firms must widen their array of innovation and development units. The main reasons to start a new 'offshore' R&D unit or to tap into Chinese universities' expertise are: (1) large and dynamic market and (2) access to local talent. Lower cost is a secondary, but welcome added benefit. On the basis of these criteria, China is clearly a location of choice. However, important requirements in this area are good-quality infrastructure and reliable enforcement of the protection of intellectual property (IP), namely patents, and court litigations on IP. This is particularly important for pharmaceutical companies, for which a strong patent infrastructure is an absolute requirement for business. Crucial to the future of China as an 'innovation-land' is the way in which the provincial courts actually put the WTO legal arsenal into practice (which has been under scrutiny since the time China joined WTO in 2001). China's domestic companies, either state-owned or private, are likely to constitute the key force towards making the IP scene a 'level playing field', as the cliché goes.

China must thus be viewed as rapidly developing into a 'fountainhead for innovation'. There are general areas for improvement, such as teamwork across functions and excessive 'technology-push' types of innovations. Also, Chinese companies have not moved towards a more 'open' or distributed' innovation system, relying on external inputs to a large degree. Several companies are already large global players: the better-known among these are the computer-maker, Lenovo, the telecommunication company Huawei, and the appliances manufacturer Haier. In addition, very large firms exist, especially in such sectors as food, which are not known outside China.

'China as a nation of innovators? It may not be too far off,' concludes a 2009 report 'Unlocking Innovation in China'[7] from the *Economist* Intelligence Unit. China's contributions will, indeed, concern products and services, as well as management practices and values, and new business models. The key for firms is therefore to fully leverage the dynamic Chinese market, but also to participate in this vital innovation scene, where China-grown innovations will increasingly flourish, for its domestic market, as well as for sale world-wide. From this, it follows that firms must carefully evaluate opportunities of partnering with Chinese universities' research activities. Program 211 from the Chinese government aims to build institutions of first-class quality. In addition, there is a program, started in 1999, to promote 38 universities to world-class level.

Furthermore, the public research institutes of the Chinese Academy of Sciences were reformed ten years ago. They total some 40,000 staff and are now divided into three types: (1) basic research, (2) market-oriented, for profit, contract research, and (3) non-profit science and technology institutes providing professional expertise.

And India?

When China is mentioned as an increasingly important source of new business models and technologies, the name of India is not too far away. There are many differences between the models at work in the two countries. It is not the purpose of the section to discuss them in detail. Certainly, the political systems, the quality of infrastructure (which is better in China), the prevalence of the English language in India are some of the factors for these differences. In both countries, there are very large numbers of engineers and scientists graduating every year and a lust for education.

In any case, numerous western companies have R&D laboratories in India, of various sizes, and maintain collaborations with universities in that country. By and large, these tend to be in the information and communication technologies (ICTs) and in the life sciences. As an example of the concern of policy-makers for the effective commercialization of technology, the large government laboratories, the Council for Scientific and Industrial Research (CSIR), have created CSIR Tech, a separate holding to act as a conduit for technology transfer. The CSIR organization was founded in 1942 and has 37 laboratory sites all over India, employing a total of 17,400 staff (12,000 of them have a technical background). Its official mission is 'to provide scientific and industrial R&D that maximizes the economic, environmental and societal benefit fro the people of India'.

When looking at the industrial activities in these fields, in IT services, the names of certain companies come to mind, such as Infosys and Wipro, both headquartered in Bangalore; in the pharmaceutical sector Dr Reedy is notable. The values and the extremely rapid growth of Infosys, for example, are exemplary.[8]

Infosys was founded in 1981 by seven computer engineers. Their vision for the company did not have much to do with revenues and profits, as they wanted to create the most respected company in India. For its customers, this company would deliver on promises and meet expectations. For its employees, it would create an open, fair meritocracy. For investors, it would provide consistent financial performance. Infosys got its first real break from the German technology company Bosch. The firm moved from Mumbai to Bangalore, in order to be close to this customer's data center. It subsequently carried out application maintenance and software development for General Electric, Schlumberger, Siemens, Airbus and Crédit Suisse, delivering these services out of its offices in India.

In 1993, Infosys went public at the Indian stock exchange and shifted strategy to focus on selected vertical markets. The 1991 liberalization of the Indian economy, India's plentiful, low-cost, skilled labor, and a time difference enabling round-the-clock operations for US/European companies, all fuelled the growth of Infosys and India's emerging software industry.

Customer satisfaction is central in Infosys' breakneck rate of profitable growth. Over a 25-year period, the company has successfully completed more than 20,000 projects, achieving a rate of 99.998 per cent error-free. Over 93 per cent of these projects were delivered on time and on budget, far above the industry average of 30 per cent. Such high customer satisfaction rate leads to over 95 per cent of clients coming back to Infosys for further projects. Relying on such customer satisfaction, Infosys proactively seeks to expand the scope of the work it does with existing clients, further fueling the revenues' growth. Infosys fully understands that in the business of outsourced services, lower cost alone is not sufficient. Quality, reliability, speed and customer orientation are fully part of the equation.

Western businesses must be curious about innovations in China and India, in terms of technology, but also for new ways of doing business. The West must become much less ethnocentric and more humble, in order to *learn* from emerging countries. In anticipation of the massive changes that will result from the need of a more sustainable world and the rapid development of China and India, firms must learn from universities, among other external actors, how to anticipate, understand and leverage change. A recent report states that, 'In a knowledge economy, universities are the most important mechanism we have for generating and preserving, disseminating and transforming knowledge into social and economic benefits.'[9] Given this, it seems sensible that firms should directly and proactively tap into university R&D.

Never before have non-business issues been so relevant to business. Never before have non-technical innovations been so critical to business success. These include novel business models or managerial practices, often enabled by ICTs. Therefore, firms must occasionally escape the short-term perspective and show imagination in projecting the broader range of activity in university research into new job-creating activities. A key conduit between the two partners is knowledge and technology transfer (KTT). The following chapters describe how this complex process may be most effectively carried out, using the three main vehicles of collaborative research, licensing and spinning out start-ups.

CHAPTER 2

Collaborative research between companies and universities

In innovation-led business development, a key vehicle for a firm to enhance its business is to tap into the relevant expertise of a university by funding projects carried out by a university team. This can be achieved in various ways. The most usual is to establish a contractual relationship, on a one-to-one basis, between the university and the company, towards a mutually beneficial, collaborative research activity. This mode, as well as other possible types of partnerships, is discussed in this chapter.

Taking the example of the company Hewlett-Packard, for a long time this firm has had a policy of carrying out research projects with universities. In recent times, this activity has been stepped up, while the number of collaborations with Chinese universities has dramatically increased, as indicated by Michel Benard, Director for university relations at Hewlett-Packard. This strategy has led the company to set up a unit aimed at evaluating its needs, in order to focus the search for external collaborations and make them as relevant as possible to future business development, or to best complement ongoing activities within the firm.

Before going into the different aspects of research collaborations between firms and universities, let us look at the situation of MIT in this regard, described in the website www.mit.edu. The latter claims that MIT alumni have created companies representing more than 3 million jobs and $2 trillion in annual world sales. MIT also indicates that it has carried out problem-solving collaborations with around 800 companies in industry, mostly multinational firms, mainly from the USA, but also from Europe and Asia. The same site quotes that the whole institute filed 139 patents in fiscal year 2009. This is not an impressive number in itself, but the key criterion is the quality of these patents. Out of them, 67 license deals were finalized in that same year. The 2009

R&D budget of MIT was $718 million, out of which $116 million, which represents 16 per cent of the total, was funded by industry.

This organization is not shy in proclaiming its merits and some of these statistics may be worthy of study in terms of the way they are defined. For example, it appears that the industry-sponsored research includes the subsidies given by US governments to firms to help them fund projects. This is particularly the case in defence-related topics or in the life-sciences area. If a more conservative approach is taken, the amount strictly and directly paid by firms, rather than 16 per cent, would be closer to between 6 and 10 per cent, This would be similar to the US average of 7 per cent, which is very close to what is found in Switzerland's polytechnical schools or the University of Tokyo. As in many other US universities, the lion's share – roughly 90 per cent of the research carried out – is financed by the US taxpayers.

Let us now turn to the specific aspects of the process involved in industry–university research partnerships. Several modes of collaborations exist, depending on the project, the time horizon, the specificity and the degree of confidentiality of the work to be carried out:

Unilateral firm–university collaboration

In this mode, the firm and the university engage in negotiations concerning the business objective, as well as the contents of a collaborative project. These conversations may take several weeks, even months. If positive, they result in both parties agreeing that the university research team prepares a proposal and the corresponding contractual agreement. When both parties agree, the contract is signed and the work may begin. The process sounds straightforward, but many pitfalls must be watched for along the way. Direct and ample communication is a must in any case. The various steps in this process are described below.

Firm and university align their interests

For the partnership to take shape, the first requirement is that both parties meet face to face, get to know each other and clearly see a common benefit in the project. If the firm does not know the activities of the university from earlier contacts, it will become more familiar with them via web-searches, through publications, and by meeting a faculty member, at a conference for example. Time is needed to build the required understanding and trust. This is critical, as most problems in firm–university collaborations, like is most collaborative projects, may be traced to misunderstandings which occurred before the beginning of the project.

Initial contacts between firm and university may first involve researchers, especially in sectors which are heavily science-based, such as life science. In this case, academics and the firm's management may know already each other from meeting at conferences. Thus, they speak the same language and have established a modicum of trust, so they can quickly test new ideas. University researchers, however, must be careful to preserve any possible patent position by not prematurely divulging inventions without both parties signing a non-disclosure agreement (NDA). Not every faculty member has the relevant skills or even the desire to engage in such contacts and collaborations with industry. Many consider that obtaining financial support from a private firm is inappropriate for an academic.

Alternatively, the first contact may have taken place between a firm's representative and personnel from the university's technology transfer department. In this crucial step, the latter must be an effective *translator*, negotiating between the issue presented by the firm and the capabilities of the university. In any case, it is critical that a faculty person or researcher be involved as early as possible in the discussions. Indeed, the person who will eventually be responsible for leading the project and the client company must directly discuss and agree on the nature of the issue at hand, the approach to solve it and the timelines involved.

In this type of negotiation towards collaborative/contract research, more often than not, an early step for both parties is, through exchanges and give and take discussions, together to revisit the issue at hand and *redefine* it, in the light of fresh input provided by both partners in the course of the negotiations.

In these negotiations, the university researchers involved must understand the context and the business case relevant to the work contemplated. Needless to say, the university's technology transfer office, if there is one, must be also 'on the same page' and act as a facilitating middle-person, making sure that there is a common understanding and that the work plan, objectives, and contractual conditions of the proposed project are realistic. Misunderstandings may easily occur, as academics tend to think that the firm has come to them because of their scientific excellence, while, in fact, the firm is on a quest for a competitive advantage in the markets: the science and the technology are only a means to attain this objective. It is also important that the academics do not 'oversell' their capabilities. The chances of success of the proposed approach must be clearly stated, as, in many ways, university and firm together are taking the risk of the success of the project, except the financial risk, which is solely on the firm side.

By and large, academics in the USA have an interest in establishing contact and working with firms. In any case, they are familiar with the process of applying for funding from sources external to their universities. A similar situation is found in the UK, where academics are quite apt at securing funds from the EU Framework Programmes, in particular.

In other countries, the orientation of the academic world towards the private sector is diverse and, in fact, varies considerably from university to university and from person to person. Because of their history, sketched in the previous chapter, universities first concentrate their efforts on education and research. Furthermore, universities have added the mission of technology transfer relatively recently, say in the 1970s – often later in the case of European universities.

Few universities world-wide have been founded recently enough to have had this third role of technology and knowledge transfer as part of their integral *raison d'être* and embedded in their mission from the very beginning. The Université Technologique de Compiègne, north of Paris, however, was founded in 1972, and, indeed, did have the idea that it had to have a strong orientation towards working with firms and external partners right from the start (www.utc.fr), so that technology transfer is a key mission (almost) as fundamental as education and research. This is embodied in its structures, with subsidiary units, called Gradient and Divergent, dedicated to commercializing the university's knowledge and R&D. The mindset of the majority of its faculties is that collaboration with external partners is both a *raison d'être* and a measure of success of their activity in science and technology.

This is in contrast with most French institutions, where, a very small number of universities and schools for higher education, the so-called *Grandes Écoles*, receive 6 per cent of their research funds from firms, which is the current international average, as seen earlier. Similarly, the figure is only 3 per cent for French public laboratories, the Commissariat à l'Énergie Atomique (CEA) being way ahead of most, as more than 75 per cent of its research is funded by industry.

Switzerland has two national polytechnical institutes of technology, one in Zurich and one in Lausanne, as mentioned earlier in this chapter. The latter, much more recent (it was created in the 1970s), has elected early to heavily engage with industry, much more so than its venerable older sister school in Zurich. In recent years, the latter has intensified its commercialization of technology. Each year, firms fund roughly 6 per cent of the total yearly research budget in each of the schools. This refers to funds directly paid by companies for R&D projects and does not include 'matching funds', as is often the case in universities statistics. This number compares favourably with the performance of the so-called 'leading universities' for partnerships with firms, such as Stanford or MIT. These two schools are key actors in the relatively well-performing knowledge and technology transfer system in Switzerland, as will be discussed in Chapter 6.

Among the few new universities created in the last 15 years in the world, one is Japan's Okinawa Institute (www.oist.jp), founded in 2005. This graduate university for science and technology lists contribution to regional economic development as a part of its mission, but this activity is mentioned in third position and seems fairly less important than excellence in research and education. This is confirmed when considering the profile of the institution and graduate students it aims to attract.

On the other hand, in Finland, Aalto University was officially established on January 1, 2010, as a merger of three institutions of higher education: the Helsinki University of Technology, the

School of Economics and the University of Art and Design. In this three-way merger, commercialization of technology is fully part of the mission of the new university, as a way to promote higher relevance to society. More information can be found of the university website www.aalto.fi. After Switzerland, Finland is generally considered as the most effective country for knowledge and technology transfer from universities to industry. It is worth noting that Singapore is in the process of launching a similar institution regrouping design, engineering and business. This Asian Republic is intent on commercializing knowledge and technology generated by its institutions, as will be seen later in this book. It is also very active in promoting a more entrepreneurial spirit in pupils and students, as well as in the population at large.

Coming to an agreement

University researchers and firms' representatives are the two talking partners. The knowledge technology transfer office (KTTO) checks and validates the contractual documents. One issue at this stage is to recognize that firms' issues, or 'problems' are interdisciplinary in nature. On the other hand, universities are tightly organized along technical disciplines. The firm's representatives and the university's 'middle-person' must be vigilant in ensuring that the relevant set of specialists are around the discussion table, so that the best possible solution is found.

When the negotiations have successfully followed their course – and this typically takes several months – both parties agree that the time has come to put the outcome of the discussions into a proposal. The university prepares this document, which is likely to include chapters such as: (1) purpose of the proposed work and business case for the project, (2) approach proposed to resolve the issue at hand, (3) work program for the project, (4) capabilities and past experience justifying a reasonable chance of success, including the profile of the investigators, and (5) budget and timing. Given the uncertainties typical of research activities, an over-expenditure clause may be included, which may represent 15 per cent of the project budget. This clause can be activated and the corresponding additional funds released after agreement between firms and university as to what the status of the project is and, therefore, what this additional money will be used for. Such a proposal must be concise, well articulated and make a compelling case for the project to be undertaken. It should not guarantee the result of the project. If this could be done accurately, there would be little reason to engage in this work. On the other hand, the proposal promises to carry out the project *on a best-effort basis.* Once the work is completed, the company is free to analyze whether this was the case or not.

Writing the proposal, indeed, is an opportunity for the research team to clarify its thoughts. Also, the proposal provides a tool for the firm's representatives, who have participated in the negotiation, to rally support and commitment from their hierarchical superior and, more broadly, from the management within the client firm. Building a broad ownership within the firm is particularly important in Japan. Unfortunately, this carries with it the inconvenience of taking much time, since no final approval is given until everybody's questions have been answered. On the other hand, once the decision to go ahead with the project is taken, everybody supports the project, because he or she has had a chance to participate in its definition. Thus, in case of a successful outcome for the research undertaken, the resulting changes or developments instigated by the company can be implemented smoothly and rapidly.

A companion piece of documentation to the proposal is the contractual document, which addresses intellectual property rights, as well as the administrative aspects for the proposed collaboration. This includes such items as payment schedule and jurisdiction in case of legal dispute. When both parties agree on the proposal and corresponding contract, they sign the latter and the project work may start. Models of contractual agreements may be downloaded from various websites, such as that of the UK Department for Business, Innovation and Skills (www.dius. gov.uk), which provides the well-known Lambert templates.[1] One set of guidelines concern 'The No-Nonsense Guide to Finance for High Growth and Innovative Businesses', which is a *one-stop resource* for companies looking for sources of funding to support their innovation-intensive business development plans. This

can be found at the business link website, www.businesslink.gov.
uk/no-nonsense.

The information provided at this website includes many funding sources, private as well as public, for sustainable development. For example, in the UK there is an organization called the
Carbon Trust, which financially supports firms working on technologies to reduce carbon output. There is also a range a funding
schemes for SMEs, including *innovation vouchers,* worth up to
£10,000, to help small businesses secure innovation support from
various sources, especially universities. This site provides SMEs
with advice on the best ways to assess funding needs, where and
how to obtain the right advice, as well as suggesting various
funding options and processes that are available.

The collaborative project starts

There is a risk that, soon after the agreement is reached and the
contract is signed, when the relatively intense contacts between the
two parties during the course of the negotiations is over, the university representatives will considerably reduce their interaction
with the firm, immersing themselves in the project work, without
maintaining much communication with the client. On their side,
the firm's managers in charge of following the project are busy
people and are likely to postpone taking the initiative of picking
up the phone and asking the project director how the project is
going. This 'incommunicado' period should definitely not last long
and the project director should make a point of contacting her client to maintain a free flow of communication, in addition to the
planned progress reports and meetings, provided by the proposal
and contract. Too much communication – this is rarely the case –
is better than too little, since, in this kind of collaboration, so
many misunderstandings and unexpected intermediate results
can derail the work and create concern or dissatisfaction on the
client's side. Each research project is unique and open-ended to a
large extent. Again, if its outcome was known, there would be no
need to do the project. It is critical to maintain frequent contact
between both parties, in order to avoid drifting into different perceptions of the progress of the work. The success of the project

largely depends upon the quality of the project manager at the university. On the other hand, firms often underestimate the amount of management time and energy required on their side in order to follow such partnering efforts.

If all goes well, the project is completed on time and within budget. The results may be not so positive, but, if the work has been well conducted (on a *best-effort* basis), the reasons for disappointing results may be quite legitimate ... and useful: it is very valuable to have a clear indication whether the approach pursued is a dead end. In this case, the project stops and the funds can be directed to another project. On the other hand, there may be room for further research; in this case, another, complementary phase is contemplated for the project, which is then the object of new negotiations, a new proposal and a corresponding contract.

As mentioned earlier, the computer company Hewlett-Packard, headquartered in Palo Alto, California, currently has in place more than 100 collaborations with universities world-wide. Out of these, close to 50 are engaged with universities located in China. The reasons for this are multiple: China has many good universities, often more 'user-friendly' than US universities, which tend to extract money from the firms and give the minimum in exchange. Also, China is a huge, dynamic market, which is the world's largest producer of computers. No doubt, many others will follow the example of this company in due course, as China is increasingly a source of scientific research and technical innovation, to be deployed both in the dynamic domestic market and for the benefit of global markets.

Several documents summarize the best practices and principles in firm–university partnerships. Several examples are given in notes 2, 3 and 4 for this chapter. We now turn to firms involving individual student-trainees in their R&D activities.

Students in the firm's R&D

Involving graduate students in the R&D activities of a firm constitutes another vehicle for technology transfer. As an example, every year, the German company Bosch invites close to 100 undergraduate or master's degree students to come to work as trainees in the company. They are selected and carefully guided in the course of their stay at the firm, so that they are strongly encouraged to contribute. They are given well-defined company projects and are located in offices, just like regular employees, near the managers with whom they work. Although it must be a real concern, confidentiality is often an overstated argument for firms not to go into this kind of engagement to gain fresh perspectives and knowledge.

In addition, for graduate students, France also has the Cifre program, which finances 1,200 PhD students per year. This program is administered by the Agence Nationale pour la Recherche Technologique (ANRT) (www.anrt.org). These graduate students carry out their research work in a laboratory belonging to a company. Close to half of these firms are SMEs. In Chapter 5, we will come back on the important mechanisms to have graduate students work with SMEs. We now turn to collaborations between several firms and a university.

Multilateral collaborative projects

Instead of a one-to-one research partnership, a relationship involving several firms may be pursued. In this case, a group of firms share the cost – and the risks – of the common project. Coming to an agreement involving several actors requires much longer negotiations, in order to identify the various partners and discuss with them a proposal federating the interests of all parties. If patent rights are relevant to the project, the respective non-exclusive rights must be carefully sorted out at the earliest possible time. This added complexity results in the negotiations with the partners taking much longer.

Multi-client projects

If the work at hand is to evaluate the potential of a new technology – for example, doing an up-to-date critical assessment of the potential of nanotechnologies in medicine, or comparing different products – say, the performance of solar cells under specific conditions, the multi-company partnership may be attractive to the clients. In this way, they share the cost of the evaluations. They also benefit from having access to a forum, in which the firms' representatives exchange reactions among themselves and discuss the project results with the university's technical experts. Indeed, every few months, a progress report is presented to all the representatives of the client companies in a one-day event. This includes discussions as to the next phases of the project, especially if the program has to be modified, as compared with the initial plan, in the light of the results obtained so far.

The leader of such a multi-client study must spend a considerable number of resources and amount of managerial time to ensure the client firms are informed and *aligned* on the purpose and contents of the ongoing project during its whole duration. The upside of such a mode of collaboration is that a substantial budget can be put together in this way. For this reason, this multi-client approach was pioneered in the 1960s – and often used – by the professional contract research organization Battelle-Geneva, a subsidiary of the US organization Battelle, headquartered in Columbus, Ohio. This approach is not often used by universities for R&D projects, but this collaborative mode is expected to become more widespread, as universities steadily acquire the necessary managerial skills.

European Union programs

When talking about multilateral collaborative research projects, or consortia, one must mention the European Union (EU) Framework Programmes. The ongoing Programme, the seventh in the series, covers the period 2007–2013, with a budget of €7 billion. This represents an increase of 40 per cent over the previous program, but only a fraction of what the EU spends annually for its Agricultural Policy. This budget represents only roughly 4 per cent of the combined R&D budgets of the 27 member states of the EU. The main item in this budget (around 10 per cent) concerns healthcare. Preparations are currently under way to launch the 2013–2020 Programme, with countries stating their suggestions. A recent German document called for a more streamlined and 'user-friendly' process.

The consortia funded by the Framework Programme are composed of very diverse types of partners: universities, industry and SMEs, as well as public laboratories. Two-thirds of the partners come from public laboratories and from the 4,000 institutions for higher education which exist in the EU. These partners come from very different country cultures as well, from Greece to Denmark. As a result, these consortia by far constitute the most diverse sets of partners anywhere in the world.

On one hand, this diversity represents a challenge in terms of managing the multicultural participants, since so many possibilities for misunderstandings exist. On the other hand, this constitutes the considerable asset of the *richness of diversity*, which is, in itself and when positively managed, eminently conducive to innovation.

In order to minimize 'misalignment' of the various actors participating in the project, it is critical that ample time is allowed for conversations to take place among the project participants at the early stage of defining the proposal and project work. This is usually lacking, because the participants are pressed to meet the proposal's deadline. They rush into defining the work program without fully weighing the implications for the different partners. Thus, the various types of expertise available are not leveraged in an optimal manner and misunderstandings are likely to emerge once the project has started.

The average size of projects of the European Union Framework Programmes has grown over the years, currently standing at €4.6 million, with an average of 14 participants per project. Over the years, these programs have been very successful in putting into contact and connecting researchers on a Europe-wide basis, in each of the various scientific and technical disciplines. Participating in the Programme seems quite valuable, since non-EU countries, such as Switzerland, regularly vote in favor of the substantial budget required to pay Brussels the entry fee required to be able to participate in the Framework Programmes. By and large, universities in the UK are quite effective in securing funding from these projects. This is largely due to the fact that UK universities are in the habit of obtaining external funding from different sources: indeed, they are partly evaluated on this ability. It is also due to the fact that all the calls for proposals and negotiations are carried out in English.

Such consortia have been very effective in putting in contact academics of the same discipline across Europe, as well as building bridges with firms and between firms. This is particularly valuable for the SMEs participating in the projects alongside the larger corporations. Individual partners subsequently carry out applied projects aimed at developing offerings for the markets.

In March 2010, the European Union announced a new initiative, the Strategic Energy Technology (SET), to shift the EU to low-carbon sources of energy. Part of this consists of allocating the remaining funds (€1 billion) of the energy section in the above Framework Programme to SET. This constitutes a strong invitation for firms to partner with universities in order to contribute to solving one of the world's most significant problems.

Aside from the Framework Programmes, the European Union has launched the European Research Council (ERC), which is concentrated on long-term, so-called 'fundamental' research consortia. Firms need to be aware of this research, as it may constitute today the basis of their R&D of 'the day after tomorrow'. The ERC program received 9,000 proposals in the year of its creation, 2007. Out of these, 200 were retained and funded, representing a total of €280 million. As stated on the ERC website (www.erc.europea.eu), the mission of the council is to support the best scientists in Europe active in all fields of science and engineering, as well as in the humanities, including archaeology and anthropology. It very much promotes investigator-driven, 'bottom-up' frontier research. The focus is on innovation rather than on specific research areas. The scientific quality is the key criterion. The proposals are selected through a rigorous process of review by peers from all over the world. The projects are up to five years in duration. The plan is to fund 500 projects in 2013, with a corresponding budget at that time of €1 billion, provided by the Framework Programme.

Multi-university initiatives

Conversely, another type of multilateral project is for a group of universities to form a consortium, supported by a firm, or a granting agency. In this case, more often than not, one university is designated as the leader, charged with negotiating on behalf of the group of academic institutions. This lead university may be chosen for its competence in the relevant field, or because it sees that project as particularly important and is willing to spend the (often considerable) effort involved in coordinating the effort.

This approach must be developed as a way of proposing fresh solutions for moving our economic system to a much more sustainable stage. To this end, the considerable relevant expertise available in universities must be federated. Universities must be much more proactive in forming such groups and in formulating ambitious projects in these areas. Funding for such projects will involve private and public sources. Indeed, such undertakings are likely to involve many years of effort and, therefore, will be somewhat similar to the long-term consortia discussed below.

Long-term consortia

Collaboration between universities and firms may go beyond the life of a given project (or projects). It may be an ongoing activity adopting a longer time horizon in the sense that a company (or companies) finances a multi-year project at a university or at a laboratory dedicated to R&D in the relevant area. The company typically brings the capital, while the university brings the human capacity. The activity of the dedicated laboratory is jointly managed and the ownership of intellectual property rights is unambiguously defined in advance.

Private–public partnerships

This route has been taken, for example, by the universities of Aberdeen, Dundee, Glasgow and Edinburgh, which formed, with their local hospitals and Scottish Enterprise an entity called the Translational Medicine Research Collaboration (TMRC) that is now engaged in collaborative research with Wyeth. The rationale behind this organization lies in assembling a complementary set of skills and data relative to patient population and their health history. Wyeth and TMRC share the intellectual property generated through the collaborative work and each has an exclusive right in its field (for Wyeth, therapeutic applications; for TMRC, diagnostic tools).

One example where universities are involved in an industry-wide long-term consortium is Sematech, in the USA. The latter was modeled in 1987 after Japan's practice on government-driven 'National Projects' consortia. It is based in Austin, Texas and was partly funded with federal grants until 1996. Its aim was to be an 'accelerator of the transition from innovation to manufacturing'. In 2009, Sematech' s CEO, Dan Ambrust, underscored the importance of non-industry partners for the consortium (www.sematech.org). He stressed that a critical issue is the timing of the innovation development. For this, collaboration is more critical than ever. It must be include a large panoply of players – 'fabless, fab-light' firms, device manufacturers, equipment suppliers and appropriate academics.

The new European Institute for Innovation and Technology

With its usual sense of innovation for novel institutional approaches, Europe has recently put in place the European Institute for Innovation and Technology (EIT). Instead of creating a new institution, with considerable expenses in terms of bricks and mortar, the EU has created a light organization orchestrating a *federation* of universities working with companies, in order to serve the needs of society. It then organizes the work carried out in a decentralized fashion – some people would talk of *networks*.

Projects group business, universities and research organizations for several years and participants to each project are located in the same place. EIT sends calls for proposals. They fall into various so-called 'knowledge innovation communities' (KICs). The first call for proposals was launched in April 2009 in three areas: climate change mitigation and adaptation; sustainable economy; and the future of the information and communication society. The emphasis is therefore very much on moving our economies towards a more sustainable state, with a subsequent impact on jobs and society. The first grants, each of €1 million, were made available in March 2010.

The Institute is currently governed by a board of 18 members coming from widely different horizons, in many European countries. Its initial budget is €308 million, from the EU, for the 2009–2013 period. Its small staff will have an orchestrating role, so that the formed consortia are in the best possible position to come up with research results with real impact. Based in Budapest since May 2010, its emphasis is on bridging knowledge and business-creation through entrepreneurship and excellence in research. It thus uniquely emphasizes the quality of content, as well as the relevance of the innovation from science to business. The website of the Institute is www.eit.europa.eu

The EIT underscores the importance of entrepreneurship. In the approach of the EIT, innovation and education in entrepreneurship must be fused together. Enhancing entrepreneurial spirit through educational programs is fully part of the objective of the EIT.

The consortium approach may also be used to secure financial support of a generic activity over a long period. For example, this is the model of *Media Lab* at MIT (www.media.mit.edu). Each company supports the activities of the consortium with an annual fee per year, for a minimum of three years. In addition, companies may leverage the consortium activity by additionally financing specific projects. In this approach, the risk is that firms find that the returns on their investments in a generic activity are not sufficiently focused on their primary interest. Long-term firm–university collaboration is further discussed below.

Co-location

Even in our age of internet, the proximity of different actors is important. In the old days, this was the rationale for creating science parks. Now companies and governments alike are creating locations where universities and firms, large or small, have a chance to meet, discuss, learn from each other and, occasionally, partner on specific projects.

Germany has a long-standing tradition of collaboration between firms, trade associations and universities, particularly the technical universities, their Technische Universitäten (TU).

They have a history of forming workgroups ('*Arbeitskreisen*') to carry out R&D work, addressing a given area in a series of joint projects. The themes of such groups include such diverse topics as: efficient filters for diesel exhausts, investment casting for precision mechanical parts, or nanotechnology for bio applications. The work may be technological and very applied or 'upstream' in nature, in order to explore the potential of a new field. Including 17 recently approved centers, the Deutsche Forschungsgemeinschaft (DFG) funds a total of 244 collaborative research centers, as of January 2010.

France has recently launched a program of competitiveness centers, or 'clusters' ('pôles de compétitivité'), federating various actors in the innovation process: companies, universities and public research laboratories. There are 76 of them; this seems a high number for a country the size of France. The issue in this kind of program is to have an effective management structure that ensures good alignment of the various actors along powerful lines of research.

In the fashionable and broad field of nanotechnology, one of the world's largest concentration of researchers in this area, called Minatec (www.minatec.org), is located in Grenoble, France, one of Europe's key regions for physics, electronics and nuclear research. Founded in 2006, Minatec makes use of a large site grouping of more than 2,200 researchers, 1,200 students and 500 firms. Numerous institutions have built facilities, in order to all be on the same site. Many informal exchanges thus take place, further fostered by events and conferences. These occasionally result in collaborations between firms and universities or public laboratories.

The innovation campuses of companies

The manufacturer of hearing implants Cochlear, based in Sydney, Australia, is an offshoot from a university. Its founder was head of a department at the University of Melbourne. The company now has 2,000 employees and continues its quest for innovation. It is in the process of further developing a site designed to provide an opportunity for universities and firms to meet and intensively exchange. It is hoped that this will eventually lead to the development of partnership projects relevant to the many aspects of such implants. These projects may well also be relevant to other industries. The point is to create a vibrant interaction, from which emerge projects addressing real 'needs'. See the corresponding website www.innovationcampus.com.au.

Philips, in its Eindhoven techno park for open innovation, is in a similar dynamic, but for a broader range of activities. The firm invites companies and research institutions to join it on the same site. It organizes forums and events to stimulate exchanges. This promotes interactions between various actors along the value chain, triggering co-innovations which would not be likely to emerge otherwise. One of its locations is the Innovation Campus in Bangalore, India (see www.PICBangalore.com). The Philips Innovation Campus (PIC) at Bangalore was established in 1996 as a division of Philips Electronics Ltd, owned by Philips Electronics NV. On this site, 1,600 professionals work on software engineering, information systems, architecture design, programming and testing. This site has steadily increased its contribution to Phillips' activities in the broad area of information technology.

The Finnish company Nokia uses co-location by creating a cadre of small R&D units close, but separated from, a number of selected universities in the world. These include Cambridge and the Swiss Federal Institute of Technology in Lausanne (EPFL), in Europe, MIT and Stanford, in the USA, and Tsinghua in China. Each unit allocates fewer than 20 research staff and rotation of personnel is orchestrated between these laboratories and those of Nokia in Finland. The growing number of offers from universities for space on their campus demonstrates the validity of such an approach. In addition, workshops involving staff from laboratories of the same firm on various campuses would help optimize their output. First, common managerial issues affecting this type of campus laboratory could be discussed. Second, researchers from the various sites could meet, in order to get to know each other and, in the course of their conversations, possibly generate ideas for business development activities.

In the case of a firm establishing an R&D unit near a university, this unit has a location distinct from that of the academic laboratory. As a rule, the university does not wish to have employees of a firm freely walking around the university premises and, for confidentiality reasons, the firm does not want open access to academic researchers. The idea is to be close by, but facilities are *separated* and the staff clearly identifiable. Meeting at the cafeteria, for example, can be the occasion for fruitful discussions, but staff must be clearly cautioned about the *really* confidential issues, which should not be touched on in these conversations.

Co-location evokes the cities from Roman times or from the Middle Ages, where the leather or weaver artisans worked side by side in one neighbourhood, with their colleagues from the same occupations. Meeting colleagues and exchanging news about people and their trade reinforced the feeling a being part of a community and encouraged the sharing of ongoing developments and activities.

For the purpose of broad exchanges of ideas, we are barely at the beginning of the effective use of electronic communication technology, which is very appropriate for such transactions. Information technology is very useful to identify an area of common interest, which can then be pursued with a meeting or by telephone conversations, which allow more exploration of potential common ground. It remains to be seen how ICTs will, in fact, truly 'globalize' exchanges of this kind, which, so far, have required geographical proximity. We will come back on this in Chapter 7.

Joint laboratories

Another model involves a joint venture between a university and a firm. One example of this kind of long-term collaboration is the nanotechnology laboratories being currently set up by IBM and the engineering school ETH in Zürich. This $90 million investment will benefit from ETH paying half of the cost of equipment and committing to a minimum of a ten-year collaboration. Its rationale is that electronic components in future computers are expected to largely draw on nanotechnologies. The agreement carries a non-exclusive use of the research results (www.micronano.ethz.ch) and relies on the achievements of the small IBM Zurich Lab. The latter received several Nobel prices, the most recent ones, on supraconductivity, were given to Drs Bednorz and Mueller.

Similarly, in France, several large companies are partners of joint public–private laboratories. For example, Saint Gobain, the world's largest producer of glass and engineered materials, operates a dedicated laboratory together with the government research organization Centre National de la Recherche Scientifique (CNRS). Created in 1990, the laboratory for R&D on interfaces and glass surfaces is housed on Saint Gobain premises and counts 15 research professionals, supported 50/50 by the CNRS and by the firm. It would take a careful study to see how truly effective such joint laboratories are in generating high-impact innovations, as opposed to opportunities for exchanges on technical issues which do not involve joint-funded ventures.

On the other hand, one of the world's leaders in building materials, Lafarge, has in place a framework agreement with CNRS, which speeds up the collaborations between the firm and the various laboratories. This followed the development of two breakthroughs, carried in collaboration with ten different CNRS laboratories: Ductal, an ultra-high-performance concrete which allows the building bridge structures as thin as those of high-performance steels; and Agilia, a range of self-placing and self-levelling concrete formulations. 'Hi-tech' innovations are indeed not only found in the IT and microelectronics sectors, but also in so-called 'traditional industries'. They require persistence over long time periods and often result from effective ongoing collaborations between firms and university R&D or public laboratories.

Embedded laboratories

Another model for tapping into university research is for a firm to lodge an R&D unit on the premises of a university. This may require care in making sure the firm employees and the university staff know who is who, as both may be a bit apprehensive about the others having free access. This model has been used at Cambridge University, where, for example, Hitachi established, 20 years ago, a small research unit at the Cavendish laboratories; the laboratory of arch-competitor Toshiba is not far away. Reporting to the corporate R&D department in Tokyo, the Hitachi Cambridge laboratory aims at creating new concepts in advanced electronic/optoelectronic devices. This small laboratory specializes in advanced measurement and characterization techniques, in close interaction with the university's activities.

On occasion, western companies make use of the embedded approach in China, as a way to have access to the talent and innovation available in the universities there, from which close to 800,000 engineers graduate each year. For example, the Danish company Novo recently established a small unit at Tsinghua University, in Beijing. This approach offers a low-risk way to 'open the door' and observe China's scene before deciding how to go forward, possibly by committing many more resources to the partnership.

In Japan, Nestlé is the first non-Japanese company to 'embed' an R&D unit at the University of Tokyo. As of November 1, 2009, a very small team, hosted by the university, acts as an office for scouting and contracting out research projects with various departments of the University of Tokyo, but also with other institutions in Japan, primarily in the area of nutrition.

For embedded laboratories, several aspects must be highlighted. First, this unit acts in the role of a *scout*, offering a window on the university's scientific activities. Their staff must therefore be carefully screened. For sure, such outfits need to be staffed with good engineers and scientists, but they must be also especially curious and good at bridge-building communication with other R&D units, as well as with the local community and markets. Second, in our internet age, geographical proximity is still a clear advantage; this is particularly true in research activities which require probing, exploring and exchanging on a broad range of topics. Conversations leading to new ideas and innovations may be prepared and followed up with electronics communication, but they need face to face interactions too. Proximity thus provides opportunities for exploring and probing, exchanging and testing, as well as ongoing contacts over a period of time. This is a prerequisite before fruitful collaborative developments may take place. The rationale for the so-called 'clusters' follows a similar logic.

Endowments

In the USA, the president of a private university is responsible for fund-raising and this task constitutes an important element in the job description; when trustees look for a new university president ability in this area will be at the forefront of their minds. A corporation, or a rich alumnus, may decide to give a large sum of money, in order to endow a chair, either in teaching or research. Typically, such sums represent a few million $US, so revenues from investing this capital pay part or all of the salary, or the research activity, of the endowed chair. At their level, deans of departments also have this function of fund-raising.

The financial mechanism of endowments is summarized at the website www.investopedia.com. In short, endowments are assets donated to universities or colleges. These are used for buildings, or invested in the case of funds, so as to provide income to the institution. University endowment funds have rules as to how much of the capital can be spent every year; it is typically 5 per cent. In the recent financial crisis, endowments lost a substantial amount of value, therefore reducing the amount of income to be spent. Several universities, including Stanford, have reduced staff as a result.

Endowments may be specifically targeted to support scholarships, research or a professorial chair. The donor may, or may not, want to be closely involved with the choice of the research subjects or of the professor.

Donations may go to buildings or equipment. If the sum is high enough, the donor gets to have the building named after her/him. If appropriate, at a later date, the generous donating alumnus may be welcomed into the academic family by being awarded a degree *honoris causa*. The donation of goods, mostly electronics equipment – computers, video equipment, flat TV screens and the like – is particularly popular, because it is a way for the donating corporations to achieve a 'window effect', which entices the students to their brands. The hope is that students will remember them when, much later, they are managers with some responsibility.

Fund-raising in this sense is not so prevalent in Europe or Asia. Mainly, this is because that there is less of a connection between alumni and universities, in part as a result of the fact that education is provided by the government. Also, such donations do not benefit from the same tax deduction. Finally, in many countries, such fund-raising is not allowed by law.

Not surprisingly, endowments to universities often have a political connotation. In the 1980s, Japanese corporations were spooking their US competitors by taking market shares in their car and camera businesses. These companies were fairly easily enticed by the offer of endowments to US universities. To maximize the 'PR' effect, these went to the so-called Ivy league universities, not to deserving local state colleges. Was this an effective way to buy the goodwill from the public at large, which was, at the time, incensed that the Rockefeller Center had been bought by a Nippon firm? Similarly, at a political summit, Japan's prime minister of the time, Mr Nakasone, announced the goodwill gesture of Japan paying the cost of a new granting agency for brain and nervous system research, the Human Frontier Science Programme (www.hfsp.org), now based in Strasbourg, in eastern France. This agency funds neuroscience projects proposed by teams comprising researchers based in Japan, Europe and the USA. The funding comes from governments, the lion's share being from the government of Japan.

The practice of endowments mainly exists in the USA for a number of reasons. One of them is that such donations are fully tax deductible there. Private universities depend upon endowments. The richest of them, Harvard, had a $37 billion endowment fund in the summer 2008. In one year, the financial/economic crisis reduced it by 30 per cent. In the course of 2009, this has caused some people to question the stability of the business model of the US private university system.

Fund-raising by universities is increasing in Europe and Asia, partly because this is a way to enhance the degree of freedom for the university president to finance new initiatives. More prosaically, such fund-raising makes it possible to compensate for the fact that public funds often do not increase at the rate required to keep up with increased costs and/or the increase in student enrolment. Such fund-raising is possible as a result of increasing autonomy for universities, seen recently in France and, a few years back, in Japan. Some of Europe's institutions have received donations for a long time, often through the wills of individuals, although such institutions are not numerous, as they need to have enormous goodwill. One such is the Pasteur Institute, which continues to receive large sums every year from the estates of deceased benefactors.

One important aspect of endowments lies in the competitive advantage it may confer. The donating firm may thus have (1) an exclusive preview window on publications, (2) the possibility to contribute to the selection of the faculty hired for the endowed chair, or even (3) an option to negotiate a license on new inventions arising from the research carried out. A less studied effect is whether large partnerships or endowments exclude or discourage competitors to enter into partnerships with the same endowed research group, department or university.

Secondment

In *secondment,* an employee (or several of them) from a company works at a university for a number of months, in order to learn or refine a particular new technical area, while contributing her/his work to the university team. No money changes hands; it is a bartering arrangement of time traded for learning. The employee's salary continues to be paid by the firm. The seconded person must be an efficient *sponge*, so as to learn as much as possible as fast as possible. The converse scheme is also possible: a university staff person may go to work in the R&D department of a firm for some time. This practice is rarely used, partly because firms want to maintain the confidentiality of their projects and their new product development activity for new business.

Japanese institutions extensively practice secondment. For example, an employee from the Ministry of Economy, Trade and Industry (METI, formerly MITI), may move from one government agency to another. METI 'manages' the career of the individual. Similarly, Japanese companies, competing with others in the market detach some of their researchers to joint projects, likely to involve university staff. These projects have some support from public funds, mainly a national ministry, such as the METI, but, also, regional funds.

In the 1980s, when its remarkable economic machine made Japan look like it was doing everything right, a source of bewilderment on the part of the West was that arch-competitors, such as Hitachi and Toshiba, seconded teams of researchers to national projects, on varied topics, such as microelectronics, energy production or car components. These project members worked side by side for the duration of the project – two or three years – and, at the conclusion of the project, went back to their home firm. Having learned through their work at the consortium, they came 'home' to put this knowledge to work in their firm to develop new offerings, competing fiercely with other Japanese companies on the world markets. It seemed that it worked fairly well in Japan at the time. Presently, METI does not favor such consortia so much. Partly, the large companies, associated in Keidanren, thought that it was time to move on to something else. These days, buzzwords at METI are more like: 'productivity of R&D and technology management', 'clusters', and regional development', as well as 'firms–academia partnerships'.

The sequence of cooperation and competition – termed 'coopetition' – typical seen in Japanese consortia, sufficiently intrigued the USA at the time, that they modified their anti-trust law in order to make possible consortia, such as Sematech, mentioned earlier.

The practice of secondment focuses attention on the fact that people represent an absolutely crucial element in technology transfer. Technical know how is primarily held in the brains of individuals. From this it follows that the most effective way to transfer technology from A to B is to move individuals holding the relevant knowledge from A to B. This is what is done when people are hired into a new job. This piece of common sense has been clear to humankind from time immemorial. In 1756, when Prussian troups occupied the center for porcelain manufacture, Meissen, near Dresden, Frederick II of Prussia relocated some artisans from Meissen to Berlin to found a local porcelain factory.

The weight of collaborative research in universities

The fact that universities carry out research projects on behalf of companies is often touted as a 'bonanza' and a great source of funds, which could then encourage governments to reduce their support to higher education. What exactly is the situation, and how much of a financial impact do such collaborations have on universities' budgets?

Overall, in the OECD countries, only 6–7 per cent of the R&D performed by universities is financed by industry. Thus, in these countries, in average, 93 per cent of university R&D is paid for by taxpayers and non-profit organizations (foundations and the like). This includes a fair amount of seed money to bring projects somewhat closer to commercial feasibility. In the USA, companies fund roughly $2 billion of university budgets each year.

It should be noted that the amounts claimed as given for the university research budgets must be taken with a pinch of salt. While it is straightforward to have the numbers of grants secured by the university, the measurement of the research activity of a university is more challenging, because it is difficult for each faculty to estimate the amount of time actually spent 'doing research'. Does a dean put to the credit of a professor's research time the preparation and delivery of a keynote speech at a conference? How about the long meetings of expert groups convened to evaluate proposals or projects of their peers?

Cornell University's policy on firms engaging with the university

In a recent document,[4] Cornell University, in Ithaca, in New York state, outlines the conditions for firms to engage with the university. Details of this text are given below, as it exemplifies the policy aspects adopted by many universities in North America in this regard. It first deals with the sponsoring of a research projects by industry. In this case the university's office for sponsored research negotiates the contract. University researchers wanting to publish must submit their papers to the sponsor 30 days before the date of publication. An additional period of two months may be granted to the sponsor in case it wants to file a patent application.

Concerning the intellectual property rights (IPR), companies have an exclusive first option to negotiate a license to Cornell's rights in intellectual property generated in the course of the sponsored research.

Research proposals may be requested by companies with definite research plans. A formal request-for-proposal (RFP) may be sent to an individual faculty member, a research center (such as a materials research center or a center for marketing studies), or college, or to the office of sponsored programs. More often, company representatives engage discussions with Cornell faculties and staff, with a view to developing a research proposal that addresses the specific research interests of the company in its efforts to enhance its competitiveness.

In addition to the direct costs attached to a specific sponsored project, its budget also includes indirect costs, called facilities and administrative (F&A) charges at Cornell, which reimburse the university for the costs incurred to support research activities. Such overheads include laboratories and office space, libraries, utilities, insurance, security, etc.

These types of guidelines are fairly common in US universities. Their complete text does not portray an excessively user-friendly perspective to companies potentially interested in engaging into research with the university. As discussed in a later chapter, universities must find the proper balance and not project a bureaucratic or a greedy approach to collaborating with firms.

Additional information on contractual issues and guiding principles are available from the Government–University–Industry Research Roundtable (GUIRR) of the US National Academies of Sciences.[5] Indeed, these recommendations must be adapted to the particular circumstances of the country and of the two partners, industry and university.

Collaborations in non-technical areas

Firms seem rarely to tap into the non-technical knowledge of universities. By interacting with universities, managers of firms may well gain a better understanding of sociological trends such as public acceptance of nuclear energy, or genetically modified organisms (GMOs), for example. Another area is the person–machine interface, which is of interest to numerous companies and where much progress needs to be achieved; many machines seem to have been designed for the peers of the designers and not for customers.

To a very large degree, the future businesses of firms depend on societal trends and it is somewhat surprising that they do not partner with universities more in these areas. Usually, consulting firms draw on university research in the social sciences, in order to transform this research into tools, insights and concepts, which they sell to the firms. Business schools may also act as channels to disseminate the results of research in social sciences.

At present, companies draw on universities' expertise in social sciences, such as anthropology or geo-economical sciences, to some extent through informal conversations, at conferences or meetings, by reading publications, as well as, occasionally, consulting with individual faculty members. They could do more. For example, they may buy innovative concepts from universities, just the same as putting a down payment to purchase a license.

Never before have non-business issues been so important to business, as indicated in Chapter 1. In spite of this, knowledge transfer to firms in the area of social sciences is fairly rare. One area, in IT, concerns the user–machine interface. New business ideas may well be suggested by academics in the course of a conversation. Examples of such ideas include the self-service bicycles in cities and sharing cars by reserving them on internet. We need many more such ideas, if we are to reduce the energy consumption and the undesirable consequences of our present addiction to car usage. Urban planning also needs innovations from universities to provide builders and authorities with workable alternatives to the space- and energy-voracious suburban landscape we have now.

As our confusing, topsy-turvy world continues to change at high speed, firms may progressively discover collaboration with universities, particularly companies in the service sector. For example, this could involve 'ethnographic marketing', where the behavior of customers is followed over a period of time – indeed, even with their consent. This can then be analyzed to inform the design of new offerings. This way, many companies could learn how to design products for an ageing population.

By interacting with universities in social sciences firms will secure fresh inputs, while universities will gain additional windows on 'the real world', as well as some additional income. This seems to be particularly relevant to companies in the broad sector of ICT, particularly mobile telephony and mobile services. In this area, non-OECD countries are coming up with breakthrough ideas; suffice to mention, for example, the possibility of borrowing $500 by mobile phone in Kenya, or the rapid development of mobile telephony in Sudan, Niger and Bangladesh, among others.

Conclusion

By transferring their knowledge and technology to companies, universities fulfill one of their missions in society. This connection with companies provides a healthy stimulation to the university. In fact, it is generally considered that the better universities for education and research are also the ones which are most active in contract/collaborative research.

R&D directly funded by firms represents a small percentage of universities' research activity. This is the case even in universities presented as being most effective in working with industry. Including in the USA, the large majority of the contract research activity of research universities is carried out for government institutions, public agencies, public granting organizations, and ministries.

Firm–university collaborative research occasionally brings crucial contributions to firms, which help them go from science to business, enhancing their competitive position. This is particularly the case in the area of life-sciences and medical technology, a field of enormous importance to provide effective healthcare at a reasonable cost to the ageing populations of the OECD countries, Japan in particular, where the proportion of old to young is increasing the fastest, and where the low birth rate has already resulted in a decrease of its total population.

Firms must also be much more proactive in tapping into non-technical knowledge and ideas available in universities. Academic contributions in these areas are not enough taken into consideration, when they could help firms understand trends in the world with a broad vision.

In brief, when a firm and a university partner in research they have a panoply of modes of collaboration at their disposal. Most fall under the general umbrella of collaborative research. Given its business-development needs, the firm must select, not only the most relevant institution, but also the most appropriate mode of collaboration suiting its requirement at that particular time.

CHAPTER 3

Firms accessing university technology through licenses

In the previous chapter, we discussed how firms fund R&D carried out in universities, in order to generate outputs that may enhance their competitiveness and help them generate new businesses and profit. Whether curiosity-driven research, with impact over the long term, or sponsored R&D aimed at bringing commercially successful offerings, this activity fully remains within the mission of research typical of universities.

In contrast, licensing requires additional skills. University research produces results which serve as a basis for patent applications and licensing agreements. Next to collaborative research, licensing constitutes another key vehicle allowing firms to enhance their competitiveness by accessing technology and the resulting intellectual property generated by the university or the public research laboratories. In order to be able to sell licenses, universities must have an intellectual property (IP) position, as well as mastering the various elements required for effectively closing a deal. This implies that the university can rely on a wide range of skills and experience, including knowledge of industry and markets, as well as familiarity with the mechanism of licensing, and appropriate staff and organization, as discussed below.

As an indicator of the magnitude of the challenge at hand, one should note that a very small fraction (around 10 per cent) of universities' licensing offices, anywhere in the world, generate sufficient income to cover their costs. This is not an indication of failure, as the number of licensing deals is probably a more appropriate criterion for evaluating the effectiveness of disseminating technology. This only indicates that such activity is not likely to provide 'bonanza' income for universities.

IP-based licensing

A licensor is defined as granting a license under laws governing intellectual property (patents, designs and copyright) to a licensee. The licensee thus obtains the rights to use the IP for a specific length of time (the term of the license) and in a defined geographical territory (for example, Japan or EU countries).

Throughout this chapter, we will use the term licensing in a broad sense, covering both the transfer of ownership of IP rights (assignment) and the permission to use these rights (licensee).

Licensing as a profession

Selling IP-based licenses, or, indeed, selling the IP outright, requires that the university has an orientation (some would say a 'culture') geared towards patenting. The university also needs to have the know how and experience to prepare, file and defend a patent application; alternatively, they can deal with an outside patent agent. Second, the licensing unit must possess a good knowledge of the industry and markets. Third, it has to have the capability to conduct negotiations on licensing scope, fees and royalties. This demands a fair knowledge of the value the patent may have in these markets, as well as of the licensing mechanisms.

Licensing thus represents an activity quite different from carrying out R&D projects. In spite of this, most research universities' members practice licensing as a channel for technology transfer.

The professional associations – in the USA the Association of University Technology Managers (AUTM), and in Europe the Association of European Science and Technology Transfer Professionals (ASTP) – direct their activities mainly towards staff of university technology transfer offices. In the case of the ASTP, 90 per cent of its members practice some kind of licensing activity.

More generally, people practicing licensing are a recognized category of professionals grouped in the Licensing Executives Society International (LESI) (www.lesi.org). This organization, headquartered in London, has 32 national and regional branches world-wide. It facilitates exchanges of experience between its members, and organizes courses on the practice of licensing, as well as conferences.

University licensing represents a fraction of total licensing activity

In order to put university licensing in perspective, it is useful to remember that the world's licensing income represents in excess of $150 billion per year. Of this, the USA secures the lion's share ($63.3 billion in 2008) and thus enjoys a comfortable surplus between the licenses sold and those bought by the USA. As compared to this number, US university licenses represented $3.4 billion in 2008,[1] a relatively small but not insignificant amount.

There is a lag between the time the licensing deal is signed and the time when the royalties become a substantial stream of income for the licensor. Thus, today's statistics from a KTT office that has recently undertaken a number of licensing deals only represent a precursor of the future flow of royalty income.

Paralleling the growth of trade, licensing across borders world-wide has considerably increased in the last decade. Most of this trade takes place between firms. As indicated above, the income resulting from the sale of licenses by universities represents only a small fraction of the total licensing trade and it is unlikely that this situation will significantly change in the foreseeable future. As the overall licensing traffic increases, the university component will more or less ride that growth, while possibly increasing its overall share of the total. It should be noted, however, that in the case of university license deals, it is their share that is likely to increase rather than the flow of royalties, since university licensing generally covers early-stage technology, whose corresponding financial compensation is small, compared to later stage, firm-to-firm licensing. University licensing managers conclude ten to twenty license deals each year, which is a larger amount than their industry counterparts.

Universities, and society at large, however, should thus not consider the sale of IP-based licenses as offering a 'bonanza' income that would significantly help balance the university budget.

Nevertheless, licensing is one of the ways for the university to make available to society the fruits of the intellectual property it generates.

Furthermore, one should distinguish between university inventions and patent ownership. Contrary to the situation in the USA, in Europe frequently the invention is made by university staff, but the corresponding patent is filed and owned by the firm funding the research. This allows the transfer to take place, but lowers statistics on the innovativeness and contribution of universities.

In 2008, Northwestern University, in Chicago, received the highest amount of license royalties – more than \$400 million.[2] This is the result of an exclusive agreement with the pharmaceutical company Pfizer for the epilepsy and pain drug Lyrica. Royalty income varies over the years, depending upon the commercial value of the product. The second highest recipient is the University of California, with \$146 million.[3]

Despite such 'one off' successes, the performance of a technology transfer office must be measured by other factors such as the number of license deals made, the amount of private investment (inside and outside the university) made by companies in licensed universities technologies and their appreciation of doing business with the office.

One university is generally considered among the world's more effective in licensing. It is Stanford University, in Palo Alto, California. Let us look at this particular example in the following section.

Licensing at Stanford University

The Office for Technology Licensing (OTL) at Stanford University was created in 1970 and has been considered an effective model of licensing organization. What are the key elements of its success?

Clearly, the combination of entrepreneurial researchers and a very active innovation-hungry region surrounding the university makes Stanford a very particular and suitable environment for maximizing efficient technology transfer out of academic research. This almost unique combination (maybe the Boston area can claim a similar situation) means that it is difficult to replicate. There are, however, a few elements that stand out and can be translated and adapted in many other operative knowledge and technology transfer offices.[4,5] They are as follows:

- Focus on marketing instead of administrative or legalistic approaches. The choice of the persons handling the technology transfer cases is essential and Stanford decided to look for people with good marketing and communication skills. The administrative work is delegated to support staff and the more legalistic issues are dealt with outside counsel. The core of the operations is run by deal-makers that have marketing and communications skills combined with academic and industry backgrounds.
- Empower the licensing officers. They are usually following a case from beginning to end and are able to work without direct supervision. They assume complete responsibility until the execution of the agreement, which is done by the office director or the vice president for research. The policies are light and meaningful. Through a flexible approach in the negotiation, they are able to act quicker and more efficiently in striking an agreement with their firm's counterparts. Teams meet up on a weekly basis to discuss ongoing cases in order to make sure that everybody shares the same understanding and has access to others as sounding boards.
- Do not focus on the money but try to plant as many seeds as possible and maintain good relationships with researchers and companies. Many deals that brought back a lot of money were negotiated with a rather conservative amount of royalties or stock. It is the wide acceptance of the technology (Cohen-Boyer gene splicing technology or Google search engine) that made the financial returns, not the amount of royalties. It is always better to have a small amount of a large pie than a large amount of a small pie.
- Maintain a balance between licensing technology and negotiating industrial-sponsored research agreements. Despite several different approaches taken on the localization of the industrial contracts office (within the sponsored research office or within the technology licensing office), separate personnel are employed to manage industrial-sponsored research contract and licensing contracts. This could be seen as a drawback from the firms' perspective but it allows the full resources of the technology transfer

operations to be dedicated to its main tasks. This avoids the risk of a gradual shift from technology transfer to industrial-sponsored research contracts in offices dealing with both tasks, which can occur due to the often more urgent aspects of contracts research negotiations.

Keeping in mind the fact that OTL has been engaged in technology licensing exclusively for almost 40 years of operations, one can draw interesting insights on the metrics and benchmarks of what is also called the 'push activity' of technology transfer, because the academic institution pushes its discoveries and inventions into the private sector. Stanford uses the services of an external patent office to file and handle the patent application and granting process.

In terms of inventions, Stanford generates one disclosure per $2.5 million of research funding. Since inception, on a total of over 6,500 disclosures received as of 2007, three (0.05 per cent) made big returns (Cohen-Boyer recombinant DNA, functional antibodies, Google), that is, over $50 million each of cumulative royalties received. Fifty-three (0.8 per cent) brought a sum exceeding $1 million. 80 per cent of disclosed inventions did not bring any revenues.

The main conclusions from the above statistics are that the OTL team has been expending a lot of effort on unproductive disclosures and obtained most of its return from only a small number of cases. Despite these sobering numbers, the overall situation is, however, very satisfactory, with a licensing income of more than $1 billion in royalties ($345 million not counting the top three disclosures mentioned above) received so far.

This impressive success, in terms of royalties collected, is made possible by the combination of three main factors:

- The quality of the inventions disclosed. This depends on many factors such as the stage of development of the invention, the width of the applications and the need for such innovations in the marketplace.
- The absorptive capacity of the firms and the competencies of the technology transfer professionals involved on the university and the firm sides. The firm should employ knowledgeable

and dedicated personnel able to identify and evaluate valuable inventions and engage with their academic counterparts. Both agents need to be deal-makers and able to structure a contractual relationship that is in line with the stage of development and the invention's potential.

- The ability of the licensing firm to bring new technology-based products onto the market. Once licensed, it is up to the firm to develop and successfully bring the product to the marketplace. Often the firms will sub-license the technology to third parties that will pursue the commercialization effort. Sometimes the company may decide to shelve the technology (existing competing products within the firm, lack of resources, etc.). All these factors make it very difficult to predict the ability of a firm to succeed in this endeavor.

In the case of Stanford, being in the heart of a region focusing on developing innovative technologies maximizes these factors. Academics work on basic research that tends to generate more disruptive innovations which have a stronger impact than incremental improvements. Researchers and technology licensing professionals are also daily in contact with the latest technological trends or developments (through personal contacts, newspapers, events, etc.), which help them to identify and evaluate promising research results. In the vicinity, a dense network of firms with large absorptive capacity for new technologies operates which maximizes the likelihood of attracting and successfully concluding licensing deals.

Is technology push (i.e., licensing new inventions out from research institutions) a luxury reserved for a handful of universities that happen to combine the necessary but exclusive ingredients depicted above? To answer this question, one has to examine the benefits of technology push, not only in terms of royalty flow back to the university, but in a more general perspective.

- A successful licensing activity helps recruit, retain and reward researchers for which not only the generation of new knowledge but its conversion in new products/innovations matters.
- Licensing activities often generate other channels of interaction with firms, such as sponsored research aiming at moving the research on from where the invention originated.

- Among all the formal (contractual) interaction channels between firms and academia, licensing provides the most 'arm's-length' relationship, particularly suited for institutions focusing in basic research.
- Licensing is the main vehicle for the creation of university spin-offs, a major source of private investment in new companies, generating jobs and increased economic development.
- Financial benefits extend beyond the university to provide regional/national governments additional tax based on the increased sales originating from licensed discoveries.
- Companies can access scientific advances and, when necessary, their related IP rights under fair and non-discriminatory terms, allowing them to invest further in their development in order to bring new products/services of added value to the public.

Most university offices for technology licensing do not perform as well as Stanford, partly as a result of their environment. The ingredients of an effective OTL, however, are similar and outlined below.

Elements of an effective technology licensing office

Looking at the example of Stanford, a university aiming at successfully selling licenses to industry needs to have the following:

- A research activity attuned to generating patents covering inventions and new concepts for commercial use.
- Effective patent preparation and filing, often carried out by a patent firm outside the university, as well as resources to pay the corresponding costs and fees.
- A market-oriented licensing office with many contacts with industry and markets.
- Capacity to negotiate licensing agreements and to close deals in a flexible manner.
- Access to and proximity of investors.
- An environment eager to have access to novel products, services and practices.

This set of requirements is a tall order for a university, especially if they are not based in a region so dynamic in the area of commercializing of technology. In fact, many corporations, in spite of their considerable resources, do not have a satisfactory licensing unit. They could call on the services of an external, specialized firm. In general, companies do not practice licensing as much as they could, despite the fact that this would provide a substantial source of income, albeit only occasionally. An example is IBM; in recent years it has stepped up its efforts to sell licenses and, as a result, secures considerable income each year – roughly $1 billion in 2008. This figure, however, includes the intellectual property fees obtained by IBM consulting, which is associated with the selling the licenses. Let us look at the various elements in licensing.

Patenting

What is key is not only to apply for many patents: the important point is to obtain patents which make sense as a basis for supporting or enhancing a business position in the word's markets. Innovation index studies typically use the number of patents obtained per year as an indicator. At best, this is a very crude indicator, since it is much more preferable for a university to focus on attractive patent applications, providing the basis for solid new business activity, rather than having a multiplicity of patents, or patent applications, which are going to stay in a drawer and cost large amounts of money to prepare, file and pay the patent fees on in different countries. This is especially challenging to universities active in basic research, for which long-term applications can be difficult to envision. The university research must thus be sufficiently connected with the market, so that it may have a reasonable chance of coming up with 'useful' patents and screening out other innovation disclosures.

Patents are valid for 20 years from the date of first filing. Some extension may be granted if the product (usually a drug) presents a special advantage. It takes two to five years to go from filing to granting. The initial filing is done in a national office. International filing may be done through a patent cooperation treaty (PCT), administered by the World Intellectual Property Organization

(WIPO), in Geneva. The overall cost of preparing, filing and maintaining (yearly fees) a patent in the industrialized countries of the world varies somewhat, but it is roughly €180,000 over the 20-year lifetime of the patent. This amount varies in magnitude, depending upon the field and the complexity of the situation.

It has been argued in some quarters that patents are actually a hindrance to innovation. Some aspects of the debate will be discussed in the following section on the business of IP. The case is not clear-cut, as the situation much depends on the industrial sector. In the present business model of the pharmaceutical industry, patents constitute a crucial business tool.

Indeed, some of the successes of licensing from university/public research concern life sciences and this sector of pharmaceutical-biotech-medical technology is particularly attentive to securing strong patents, because it is a key basis for its business. When the patent protecting the new drug expires after its normal life of 20 years, the drug becomes a generic, which means it can be sold by other firms. This causes the price of the drug to drop to a fraction of its value in a matter of a few weeks. Without some kind of temporary exclusivity, no pharmaceutical company would have any incentive to spend the large sums necessary to develop new products and obtain drug approval in the first place.

Another example in this area is Taxotère, a leading drug for treating various types of cancer by chemotherapy, discovered by CNRS researcher Pierre Potier. As is often the case, this passionate researcher was motivated in part by the fact that his spouse had cancer: After many obstacles, administrative and otherwise, he managed to launch his discovery onto the market via the company Sanofi Aventis.

In the USA, some 180,000 patents are granted each year. As mentioned in an earlier section, IBM is a major recipient of US patents. When it comes to patenting practices, the Court of Appeals for the Federal Circuit, created in 1982 in Washington DC, has jurisdiction over patents and trademarks (www.cafc. uscourts.gov). Its rulings influence the approach of corporations towards patents and litigation. For example, recent rulings (such as *Seagate*) were carefully analyzed; there is a case for increasingly discouraging companies to initiate litigation, which is big business in the USA, but does not create much value for society.[6]

In addition, an overhaul of the US Patent Office was announced and the US Supreme Court has rendered judgments making it less likely to patent so-called 'obvious' matter, slowing somewhat the growth in low-quality patent applications. This, as well as other measures, constitutes what is sometimes referred to as patent reform. In this connection, the US Patent Office (www.uspto.gov) has recently launched an electronic forum to gather feedback and comments from the various stakeholders on the quality of patents and on possible reforms.

In less rich countries, good university research is some-times literally pilfered by institutions from rich countries, for at least two reasons. First, the universities in countries, such as Cameroon or Ghana for example, typically do not have much in the way of resources for preparing and filing patents. What is required is ability to train and certify good patent lawyers and technology transfer professionals, who can identify and protect promising technologies, with the support of third parties. Geneva-based WIPO (www.wipo.org) and its sister African organization Organisation Africaine pour la Propriété Intellectuelle (OAPI) (www.oapi.org) are trying to mitigate this situation. This is done by providing funds and professional help to file patents. Second, in those countries, university research teams are so starved for funds that, if a company, a foundation or a university from the West funds a research project, the team will be so glad to receive some cash for equipment and consumables, that it will give away all the project's results lock, stock and barrel.[7]

Licensing practice

A patent position is a prerequisite before contemplating the option of selling a license. First, does this patented innovation lend itself to licensing? Let us assume, as is generally the case, that we are dealing with a product patent. Many items need to be negotiated with the potential client, which requires substantial preparation work. What is the size of the market concerned by this innova-tion? What is the geographical scope considered? What are the dynamics in terms of market: demographics, societal trends, regulation, environmental concerns. Crucially, what is the range of expected cost to produce the new product? In the industry of interest, what are the practices regarding the level of royalty – 5 per cent or 10 per cent of the selling price of the product? Is an upfront license fee appropriate; if so, of what amount?

Initially, negotiations can take place with several prospects, in sequence and in parallel. It is well advised to first approach a prospect that is not a leader, so as to sharpen the business case in such practice negotiations. In most cases, though, the first approach is actually made with the most promising prospect. In any case, the process takes time and resources, since the potential licensees can be anywhere in the world.

It is possible to include a licensing clause in contract research, described in the previous chapter. After the project phases of feasibility and early development, funded by the client firm, the latter is better placed than a university to carry out the scale-up and, of course, the manufacturing and distribution of the new product. In order to fully capture the value of the innovation, the university may be able to receive a royalty income on the commercialized products, and/or a licensing fee. It is, however, cumbersome to negotiate such a licensing deal at the time of the proposal and before the research project itself is carried out, that is, when not much is known about the real potential and the expected cost range of the new product. This does not give a very strong negotiating hand to the university.

Again, in the USA, the 1980 Bayh-Dole Act prevents universities from selling the patents outright. They can only sell rights, exclusive or non-exclusive, on the use of the university patent. In contrast, European universities may either license or sell the intellectual property itself. In any case, there are very different ways to approach licensing, as indicated in the AUTM website (www.autm.net). The appropriate approach depends upon the institution and on the specific circumstances of each invention.

The business of IP: patent aggregators, patent trolls, and patent pirates

A couple of decades ago, it was usually considered that roughly 80 per cent of firms' assets were tangible and 20 per cent intangible.

Following an increase of intangible assets, for around 80 per cent of US-listed companies (in 2007), the figure is now closer to a 50 per cent split for firms listed on the AIM stock exchange (for smaller growing companies), as of March 2009.

The rapidly growing role of intangible assets has inspired a series of business models focused on intellectual property. Among these models, the term 'patent troll' has been used for companies that build and exploit a patent portfolio to engage in litigation (assert their patent rights) against companies active in the marketplace. The specificity of patent trolls is that they operate specifically on the IP front and do not practice nor develop their inventions. In short, patent trolls buy IP in order to be able to sue firms with deep pockets. The threat of a suit may well result in a settlement out of court, which may also be lucrative for the patent troll company.

Non-practicing entities (NPE)

Since it may well be difficult to distinguish companies that unduly exploit the patent system from others that are merely trying to obtain a fair remuneration on discoveries (made by themselves or third parties), the more general term of 'patent assertion', initiated by non-practicing entities (NPEs), is usually used.

According to Patent Freedom (www.patentfreedom.com), an advocacy group tracking the intensity of patent holdings and litigation brought by NPEs, since 1985 a total of about 315 NPEs have been involved in about 3,100 cases, with 75 per cent of the suits filed since 2003. Targets are large companies principally active in telecom and software business, such as Apple, Sony, Dell and Microsoft.

As a defense against the threat of being faced with NPEs/patent troll suits, large companies are setting up or joining new entities created collectively. For example, Philips, RIM, Avaya, Motorola, Verizon, Cisco, Hewlett-Packard and Ericsson support the Allied Security Trust (www.alliedsecuritytrust.com), a not-for-profit entity, which acquires and shares patents in IT, semiconductor and software fields. Rational Patent Exchange corporation (RPX) is a for-profit defensive patent aggregator that acquired about 1,000 patents in its first year of existence and has attracted customers such as Sony, Philips, Panasonic, Samsung, IBM, HTC and Cisco. In both cases, the aggregator buys patents valuable for their considered field of business and may resell them later to third parties (which, in fact, could be NPEs) under the conditions that the buyer agrees not to assert them against any of the existing members at the time of the transaction. This makes a compelling case for becoming member early enough, in order to belong to the list of existing licensees when the patent is sold.

Intellectual Ventures (IV), one of the founders of which is a former manager at Microsoft, goes one step further than RPX, above, in the sense that it does not exclude the possibility of litigating in courts, hence could be seen as an aggressive NPE against companies which are not its customers. Its large fund ($5 billion) makes it a powerful player, able to draw large sums of money from companies, so that they benefit from the umbrella constituted by its 10,000 patent families. A recent article[8] claims that the business model of IV is fully aimed at creating value and boosting economic development.

Legal considerations

Recent court decisions in the USA have made it more difficult for NPEs to assert their rights by limiting the possibility to block early in the procedure the targeted business of the defendant (limited injunction following the *eBay Inc.* v. *MercExchange* ruling by the Federal Circuit in 2006). Large companies are lobbying the US government to change the Patent Law in order to make it more difficult for NPEs to assert their rights (see the website for the Coalition for Patent Fairness, www.patentfairness.org).

A revision of the Patent Law is being debated on the grounds that large companies, which present themselves as victims of NPEs, are seen by some smaller IP players as guilty of wrongful behavior. They are alleged to act as 'patent pirates', 'using without compensation' patent rights of small firms or individual inventors which are no match for their large size and financial resources. NPEs that help such smaller patent holders to obtain fair compensation are claimed to support innovation, contrary to the allegation of the large companies.

So, patent trolls versus patent pirates? Probably both camps bear some responsibility for excessive, or even unreasonable, use of IP rights. Large companies, by supporting patent aggregators that sell patents back to rogue NPEs, are indeed contributing to undermining innovation. Indeed, small, growing and innovative firms, which are not able to buy themselves protection from aggregating companies, will be exposed to the attacks of opportunistic NPEs. On the other hand, the growing financial backing of firms collecting mixed bags of IP rights with only the aim to go for big sums and deep pockets, blocks the diffusion of innovations from operating companies.

Implications

Why should we care? Many patent aggregators are backed by financial investors that expect to obtain their money back with interest. As an example, Intellectual Ventures, which has raised $5 billion and bought so far 10,000 patent families, needs to get money out of IP users in the marketplace. Though it has been successful in obtaining important payments from large firms, the next step will be SMEs and, when needed, litigation could be used to further 'monetize' its patent investment. For this reason, it is expected that these organizations will have an important impact on firms that are active in technological innovation (mainly IT, software and communications). Firms need to develop and carefully scrutinize their patent portfolio to minimize the risk of being confronted by financial claims from an NPE. In order to do that, firms should move away from filing too many (defensive) patents, since they are not effective against NPEs. Instead, they should involve their R&D departments early in order to monitor better the risk of being the victim of NPEs' patent assertions.

As a source of numerous basic and far-reaching patents, academic technology transfer needs to be careful in avoiding supporting patent trolls or pirates; they 'would better serve the public interest by ensuring appropriate use of their technology by requiring their licensees to operate under a business model that encourages commercialization and does not rely primarily on threats of infringement litigation to generate revenue'.[9] From firms' perspective, some of them, mainly in the USA, are beginning to report stopping certain specific areas of R&D because of the threat of possible actions on the part of patent trolls.

By and large, Europe seems to be much less affected by patent trolls or pirates. Only a few companies act as NPEs. Names such as Sisvel (subsidiary of Philips), IP-Com or E-data have engaged into legal battles against operating companies. The main reason for this discrepancy is the different legal framework, making such actions more difficult and less rewarding. Firms must, however, keep in mind the growing market for such players and the pressure they will have, as they bring hefty returns to their investors. As examples, Intel had to pay Intergraph $675 million and Assure Software received $100 million on one patent. In the case of NTP against RIM, under the threat of injunction, RIM settled for the hefty sum, of $612.5 million.

Even a public research institution, however, the French Commissariat à l'Energie Atomique, mentioned in the previous chapter, is keeping control over its own patent portfolio, in order to attract large sums of research collaboration money from firms looking to benefit from this institutional umbrella against potential infringement suits. The aggregator Open Innovation Network (www.openinnovationnetwork.com) focuses on building cross-licensing arrangements for commercial companies, in exchange of free access to its own patents.

Losing sight of common sense in granting patents for licensing

On occasion, the granting of patents seems to make no sense at all. Let us look at the case of basmati rice.[10] This long-grain rice has been grown in India for centuries. The word 'basmati' means 'queen of fragrance' and this type of rice has come to be in great demand all over the world. An agricultural company in Texas, RiceTec, developed, trademarked, and obtained a patent on new strains of basmati rice in 1997 (US patent 5,663,484). This patent could possibly have had huge significance for India, since farmers of that country would then have to pay royalties to that company. By what twist of the legal procedures could a patent on basmati rice be granted on a product known for centuries in India? On hearing about this, the Indian government lodged a protest and basically obtained an annulment of the patent from the US Patent Office (USPTO). Its position was that long-existing strains of rice presented the same characteristics as the patented form. The term 'basmati' was maintained by the US Federal Trade Commission, whereas, the UK Food Standards Agency recognized in 2002 that the name specifically designates rice varieties recognized as such by Indian and Pakistani authorities.

A similar instance again occurred concerning the use of turmeric for the healing of wounds. There, also, a patent was granted in the USA and the Indian government attacked it, prevailing in annulling the patent on the grounds that the practice had been well known in India since time immemorial.

A positive example of licensing between a western company and a non-OECD country concerns Costa Rica. In 1991, the large US pharmaceutical company Merck signed a contract with the non-profit organization Instituto Nacional de Biodiversidad (INBio). According to the contract, the Institute would provide 10,000 plant samples over a period of two years, together with the information on their traditional usage. For this, Merck paid $1.35 million to INBio and agreed to pay 2.5 per cent of royalties on any drug that emerged from any of these plants.

The difficulty of licensing public research: the case of BTG

One example illustrates the challenge represented by doing a profitable business from a licensing activity over a long period. In 1948, the British government founded the National Research Development Corporation, which was merged in 1981 with the National Enterprise Board to form the British Technology Group (BTG); its brief was to commercialize the results of public research, essentially through licensing. In 1986, the government abolished BTG's monopoly for that mission, in an attempt open up the game and to make the technology transfer more successful.

For example, MRI was a technology first licensed by BTG in the 1980s. BTG experienced a number of difficult phases financially.

After a management buy-out in 1992, it transformed itself into a specialty pharmaceutical company, with several products in trials and an active in-licensing activity to enrich its portfolio of drug-development projects. In 1995, BTG plc was listed on the London Stock Exchange. In 2005 it announced that it was to divest its interests in the area of physical sciences to concentrate on life sciences. Since then it has licensed several products and made acquisitions, the most recent one being Protherics in late 2008.

Universities need clear ownership of intellectual property

The previous paragraph mentions the relatively intricate negotiations required in selling IP-based licensing. A prerequisite to entering the negotiations is that the ownership of the patent is clear and straightforward. This is often not the case. When several sources of monies – government, non-profit, industry – are put together to fund a research project at a university, the question 'Who owns the patent?' is often a difficult one to answer. This makes it practically impossible to complete the negotiations and, when third-party investment is sought to finance an additional phase in the development towards commercialization, a deal will not be likely to be concluded as a result of this lack of clarity on the ownership of the intellectual property. In this area, the investors want to have complete control, so as not to be impeded in the activity at a later stage.

The USA leads in this arena

In the USA, a law went a long way towards clarifying this situation. It is the Bayh-Dole Act, already mentioned. It was enacted in 1981. This law gave full ownership of patents filed in the course of research projects financed with Federal Government money.

In the USA the number of patents filed by universities has steadily grown in the 1990s and 2000s. In any given year, the leader in this field, MIT, is granted in excess of 100 patents; a similar figure is recorded for Caltech or Stanford. These are not very high numbers, but, again, the quality and the value of the patent for commercialization, are much more important than the quantity. A recent paper looks at faculty patenting.[11] However, it is difficult to assess the exact impact of the Bayh-Dole Act as an accelerator of the trend, which, it can be argued, had been taking place anyway in the 1980s. Indeed, this period coincided with the early and rapid development of the science-based biotechnology industry. This would explain why, even without this Act, there would have been a rise in the number of patents granted to universities. In the USA in particular, the prevailing model of transfer from university to companies works well in the area of life sciences, where patented products and royalty-based deals are a well-established part of the business.

In 2008, universities and public research laboratories received a total of $3.4 billion in licensing and royalty income.[12] The large increase over 2007 is due to the substantial payment by Pfizer to Northwestern University, mentioned earlier. The bulk of the $3.4 billion sum is composed of royalty income, while the sale of equity in university start-ups represents a small fraction of that amount.

Many OECD countries have passed laws similar to the Bayh-Dole Act mentioned above. However, Switzerland does not have a similar act and this seems to be no problem for a country usually rated as performing well in technology transfer (see Chapter 6). In the United Kingdom, this was done in the 1980s; in Germany, it was in 2002. The rationale is similar: streamlining and clarifying patent ownership, so the universities can best proceed with commercializing patented technology. Another such country is Japan, which has made recent efforts to connect firms and university R&D, as discussed below.

Who buys licenses from universities?

There are statistics on the various segments of companies buying licenses, and an overall conclusion is given by Geiger.[13] Large multinational corporations tend to be highly selective in exhibiting interest in early-stage technologies, since, at this point in development, it is not clear how the discovery might eventually translate into profitable business. Furthermore, as we have seen previously, firms are not always proactive in seeking partnerships with universities. On the other hand, universities strike licensing deals with smaller companies, and, increasingly, with start-ups. By and large, more than half of university licenses concern companies of less than 500 staff. Close to 20 per cent are granted to start-ups. In this case, 90 per cent of licenses are exclusive.

Developing Technology Licensing Offices in Japan

In a period characterized by an extremely short-term perspective, accentuated by the tyranny of quarterly profits, Japan is a very rare country in truly putting technical innovation for economic competitiveness as a top priority. Japanese actors of innovation are willing to invest 'patient money' for technical innovation to come to fruition. Politicians and managements of corporations, media, and society at large all have a lust for technical innovation. In fact, the *Economist* Intelligence Unit has recently declared Japan as the most innovative country in the world. In the recent past, the government has put in place reforms in order to enhance the low interaction between firms and universities in Japan. This includes the creation of 29 technology licensing offices (TLOs) in universities all over the country.

A conviction that innovation is key

In the 1990s, Japan carried out a number of noteworthy reforms. As in many European countries, however, much still remains to be done. But there is one area where commitment and leadership have been unfailing over the years, and that is that technological innovation is central to national economic growth.

For example, Japan's Schumpeterian (from the Viennese economist Schumpeter) view of the positive aspects of 'creative destruction' has prompted the country to invest more than 3 per cent of its GDP in R&D. This is the highest ratio of all the large industrial countries (except for Israel) and represents roughly €100 billion per year. Close to 75 per cent of this sum comes from the private sector – a percentage similar to that in Switzerland. For the first time in many years, these investments have decreased (by 0.8 per cent) in the fiscal year April 1, 2008 until March 31, 2009, as compared to the previous fiscal year. This is attributed to the economic crisis.

It is not, however, sufficient to pour money into R&D; it is also necessary to drive an *effective* innovation process, so as to convert these investments into commercial offerings, which can be successful on the world's markets. Japan is, indeed, working on improving this process as well – for example, by launching a massive program for training managers, as well as structural reforms, including reforming the status of universities in order to improve the currently very poor linkage with the private sector.

Strong support from the top

Another ingredient of the success of innovation policies is the effective leadership of the top politicians. Continuing the practice initiated by Mr Koizumi, Japan's prime minister chairs in person the Council for Science and Technology Policy (CSTP), once every two months. In what other country is such a commitment demonstrated at the highest executive level?

Japan's pro-innovation attitude is complemented by the fact that the president of Keidanren, Japan's Business Federation, is Mr Fujio Mitarai. The latter is chairman of the $35 billion sales company Canon, leader in digital cameras and one of the world's most effective firms in converting technical innovations into cash.

In 2007, the Japanese government formulated *Innovation 25*, a blueprint for the country, which included renewal of technology, as well as of the social system. It recommends 150 urgent measures and 30 additional longer-term steps. It is not clear what the current government is going to do with this document, which has been the object of a fair amount of debate in Japan, but the interesting thing is that the government is keen to be looking at a horizon two decades away.

In Japan close to 75 per cent of R&D investments are funded by private companies and are carried out within companies. This represents a much higher percentage than the OECD average in this area. In contrast to the USA, Japan's universities have a weak linkage with firms, at least when it concerns collaborative research and technology licensing. In an attempt to correct this, starting in 2002, laws were enacted to give more autonomy to the universities. This was part of a general effort to upgrade and reform Japan's university system. Part of this was to create TLOs in 29 universities, as mentioned above. Between them, these offices generated the modest combined license revenue of ¥410 million in 2002, which represents 12 per cent of the corresponding number in the UK. One of the most successful TLOs is CASTI, which is part of the University of Tokyo. The activities of this university will be discussed further in Chapter 4.

Japan, a model for Asia?

With its cars and cameras very successfully taking over world's markets in the 1960–90 period, Japan's spectacular economic growth has effectively leveraged technical innovations for economic development. It thus constitutes a model for Asia. South Korea has followed it, climbing the value chain even more rapidly than Japan did, and continues to forge ahead. South Korea's investments in R&D have rapidly grown between 2000 (2.5 per cent of GDP) and 2007 (3.2 per cent). The country plans to invest the world record percentage of no less than 5 per cent of its GDP by year 2012. This level is currently only attained by Israel, with Japan in second place with roughly 3.2 per cent of GDP.

Since three-quarters of South Korean investments in R&D are made by firms, as is the case in Japan, the government intends to step up its investments in long-term, curiosity-driven 'basic' research. The Korean society is already one of the world's best equipped as far as the high-capacity communication network is concerned.

Licensing in the German system for technology transfer

Germany has one of the best records for connection between firms and universities, in particular technology universities (TU).

The research scene is rather complex, as its responsibility is shared between the Federal level and the 16 Länder of the German Federation. In total, in Germany, firms contribute more than two-thirds of the overall R&D investments in the country. In the remaining third, funded publically, the Federal government invests 55 per cent and the *Länder* 45 per cent.

There are 250 universities in Germany, of which 100 are universities for applied sciences (*Fachhochschulen*). The overall budget of the Federal Ministry for Research and Education (BMFB) was increased to €10 billion in 2009. Germany had just completed a program of €15 billion in the period 2006–9 to strengthen university research and make it even more relevant to industry. The approach is also to promote nine university centers of excellence. One key objective is to increase the intensity of licensing of university research to firms.

The environment in Germany for the generation of science and technology presents a rich panoply of actors, somewhat like Japan. Next to universities, there are four non-university institutions that carry out research as well as industry: in its 15 institutes, Helmholtz, the largest player (with a budget of €2,2 billion in 2008) carries out long-term research on public interest in healthcare and energy. It is 90 per cent funded with public money, from the Federal state, as well as from the *Länder.* The Max Planck Society mostly does curiosity-driven research, with public funds (80 institutes; public funds are roughly 90 per cent of the financing, of which half is Federal and half is state funding).

The 80 Leibniz Institutes carry out diverse long-term or applied work and as, a result, receive two-thirds of their funds from public sources and one-third from third-party support.

The Fraunhofer Society (FhG) constitutes a bridge between university and public research and industry. It is discussed also in the Chapter 5 on collaborations with SMEs. The 58 institutes of the Fraunhofer Society collectively have more than 12,000 employees and did €430 million of contract research with industry in 2006. In addition, roughly €400 million come from institutional public funding. Licensing revenues were €135 million in 2005, thanks to rapid and massive developments in MP3 technology and strong activities in start-ups through the Fraunhofer

Venture Group. Like other contract research organizations, the Fraunhofer Society puts a high priority on internationalizing its activities and has been increasingly active in China over the last ten years, essentially supported by German public funds for cooperation with non-OECD countries. So far, this activity does not seem to entail any licensing deal yet.

The growing attention to technology transfer has resulted in stepping up measures in this area over the last ten years. In 2002, a Federal initiative created 21 patent marketing agencies (PMAs), of which 13 were new entities. Their function is to negotiate and finalize the commercialization deals, mostly via licensing. In Germany, the patent belongs to the institution and the researchers/professors must declare any invention to their employers, as a result of the German Employee Invention Act, which was enacted in 2002. Prior to this, university professors had an exemption and could therefore be the owners of patents.

The PMAs belong to a wider association, Technologie Allianz e.V. (www.technologieallianz.de), the German network for marketing patents to firms. It includes technology transfer offices and agencies – more than 200 institutions representing more than 100,000 scientists. Thousands of patents are available for licensing and more than 100 innovation experts are accessible to help direct firms and to negotiate deals.

Yet, another technology transfer institution is Ascenion (www. ascenion.de). Research generated in three out of 15 Helmholtz science centers specializing in life sciences, are commercialized by Ascenion, which also serves several Leibniz institutes and the Medizinische Fachhochschule, in Hanover. Max Planck Innovation plays a similar role for the 80 institutes of the Max Planck Society. Finally, Germany is on the point of releasing a contract-type form of technology transfer. The objective is to provide guidelines facilitating the establishment of firm–university partnerships in their various forms.

How about China?

It is clear that China will become a major source of innovations in the relatively near future. The question is: 'When this will actually take place?' Recent evolutions, outlined in the latest OECD country report on China[14] confirm the ambitious plans of China in this arena. We begin below by discussing, further to Chapter 1, the increasing pool of R&D activity, which will, in due course, provide a basis for future licensing revenues.

The rapid growth of R&D investments in China

China's total investments in R&D are estimated to have been $87 billion in 2006, growing by 19 per cent each year, in real terms, between 2001 and 2006. This investment is expected to continue increasing at breakneck speed. It is anticipated that, by 2020, China will double its 2006 rate of 1.42 per cent of GDP invested in R&D. In China, as everywhere else, more important than the amount of input is the quality of the output, which is difficult to truly assess and extremely difficult to predict. Part of the quality of output is, indeed, the cash generated by the commercial success enabled by the innovation. In absolute terms, the growth of the R&D investments is very rapid, given the dynamic evolution of Chinese GDP, in the range of 10 per cent per annum. A substantial portion of these investments go on equipment, with the rationale that state-of-the-art laboratory installations will attract talent in due course. The result is that, walking through these laboratories, one often is struck by the quality facilities but cannot help noticing that the buildings are fairly empty and the equipment does not appear to be much used.

Statistics indicate that, in 2008, there were over 800 R&D centers established in China by non-Chinese companies. One of the most recent was announced in 2009 by Bayer, stating its intention to open its first R&D center in Asia in Beijing. The commitment is to invest €100 million over five years in this facility. If the above number of 800 is correct, it is clear that many of these will be small 'observation posts', with no development activity at all. These R&D outposts are windows on the activities of Chinese universities with a view to engaging with them at the appropriate time. In any case, the challenge to technology companies is real: as they already struggle to make their innovation processes more effective, they face the added complexity of integrating

Asia's talent and sources of innovation into their global array of development activities. Two sectors are particularly relevant: ICT and life-sciences/healthcare. But 'greentechs' (technologies for a more 'sustainable' economy) are also of high interest. Indeed, China puts a high priority on acquiring and developing technologies which will help make our economies more sustainable. True, China emits a lot of greenhouse gases, but many countries could emulate its commitment for greener technologies.

The 2008 Chinese 'stimulus package', designed to mitigate the economic 'crisis of the century', specifically spells out the high priority put by the government on investments for R&D/innovation. In passing, it is interesting to note that all top Chinese politicians have a science or engineering degree, so that they are well prepared to understand the power of technical innovation. An estimated 15 per cent of the $600 billion stimulus package will go to fostering innovation. Although many details are not known, it seems that a substantial part will be channeled into the existing 15-year Science and Technology Plan to strengthen domestic innovation capabilities.

University licensing in China

As far as universities are concerned, the 1995 legislation opens the way towards enhancing their autonomy. They are encouraged to increase their activity in knowledge and technology transfer to firms. The Chinese government allows the commercialization of intellectual property resulting from work carried out under government funding. The relatively modest sum of an estimated €20 million (RMB200 million) of licensing income, was generated by universities in 2005.[15] In 2001, in order to accelerate the licensing activity of universities, national technology transfer centers (NTTC) have been created in six universities: Tsinghua in Beijing, Jiotong in Shanghai, China East Polytechnic, Huazong, Jiaotong in Xi'an, and Sichuan University. Since then, the situation has evolved, but it will take a while for this vehicle for technology transfer to really have an impact. The basic elements, however, are in place to participate in a continuing rapid growth of technology transfer activities. By and large, in China, the university owns the patent, even if a firm has paid for the collaborative project during which it has been filed.

China's Science and Technology Development Law of 1993 lays the foundation for putting science and technology on top of the list as an engine for economic growth. It also allows better connections between industry and universities, which, up to 1993, had been two totally separate entities.

Concerning the output in scientific papers, China has rapidly increased its share of the world output from 2 per cent in 1995 to be 9 per cent in 2008, which is similar to the UK. The fast ascent is, indeed, due to the remarkable increase in R&D investments. It is also partly due to the fact that China is giving incentives to academics to publish papers and to write them in English. Observers argue about the level of quality of these papers, in comparison with international standards.

Intellectual property

With regards patenting, with its entry into the World Trade Organization, China aligned its patent laws with international standards. In 2005, the crude indicator of patents granted gives a total of 21,000 science and technology patents obtained, roughly ten times the number ten years before. A comprehensive web journal, *Managing Intellectual Property* (www.managingip.com), focuses on patent issues.

The courts are unevenly, but gradually, enforcing a more western approach to patent litigation, but large domestic players, such as Haier, TCL, Huawei, CHINT group and Lenovo, not to mention smaller, but emerging firms, are as likely as foreign companies to push for 'even-handed' litigation, so the situation is expected to continue improving.

China, soon the laboratory of the world?

As with everything else in this enormous and extremely dynamic market, China is now poised to become a key player on the world innovation scene. The unknown is the rate at which this evolution will take place. The guess is that it will be a sustained rhythm, which is likely to be accelerated by China's policies and investment following the ongoing 'once in a century' financial and economic crisis. There are barriers in this development, such as the general lack of teamwork in the laboratories and the insufficient level of managerial sophistication, not to mention possible corruption issues. China, however, is learning fast, in part from the example of western companies presently in the country, but also from the diaspora of managers and students coming back from abroad to find employment among the opportunities offered by the country. It is estimated that each year, about 100,000 oversees Chinese students and professionals come back to China. The country has a comprehensive program to support students in overseas universities, provided that they come back to the home country.

Whenever China accedes to the status of being a major source of innovations, it will benefit the whole world, but it is also a healthy stimulation for the economies of the West, as well as Japan and India, encouraging them not to allow themselves to become complacent, keeping up the pressure on them to pursue appropriate reforms. Also, this development will push non-Chinese firms to increasingly engage in technical developments with Chinese partners, universities among others. The fact that China has become a major player in the world's innovation scene should be viewed positively: by analogy, the rise of Europe in this scene after World War II did not represent a problem for the USA. On the contrary, it enlarged the level of activity for everybody concerned.

Turkey

With its large and rapidly growing population, Turkey has a dynamic economy attracting a fair amount of foreign direct investment (FDI). In 2005, the government started a process of formulating a comprehensive innovation strategy for the country. It called on the collaboration of Turkish academics, as well as European experts. The resulting blueprint calls, in particular, for much stronger partnerships between industry and the many universities present in the country, especially in the Istanbul area.

More information may be obtained at the website of the Science and Technology Research Council of Turkey, Tubitak.[16]

Conclusion

In brief, in order buy licenses from universities, firms must partner with institutions having the following capabilities:

- high-quality research;
- a range of specialized skills, which typically are outside the range usually available at universities;
- good knowledge of firms and markets – world-wide.

For universities, licensing usually represents a relatively small proportion of their income, as compared to the cost of running a TLO, and very small indeed, as compared to the total cost of research in a university. So, why bother? Selling licenses represents the following:

- part of the mission, next to teaching and research;
- a way to recruit, reward and retain researchers;
- a privileged technology-transfer channel for basic research institutes;
- a vehicle by which to interact with firms;
- a source of economic development – for example, through contributing to the firms' competitiveness or spinning out new ventures;
- a necessary exercise for knowing the 'real world', regardless of cost;
- a substitute for the absence of long-term, curiosity-driven research in corporations;
- a welcome (small) source of discretionary cash for the university;
- proof of relevance for society.

The rationale for each university to engage in licensing is composed of a different mix of the above factors. Above all, it is contemporary 'common wisdom' that universities must be more connected with and relevant to firms. More than the monetary aspect, universities see licensing as part of disseminating the results of their research.

Technologies towards a more sustainable economy provide universities with a substantial scope for generating and licensing innovations – and for changing the world for the better. Together with collaborative research, selling licenses is one key vehicle for engaging with firms. Each university has to decide how much it wants to commit to each of these types of vehicles.

By and large, licensing is expected to continue to increase in the foreseeable future, as a component of a generally expanding technology trade. China and India will enrich that field, as they progressively come on stream as welcome additional and original sources of innovations. In the not too distant future, their contributions may well be leading the world in specific areas.

Universities are expected to follow this licensing trend and participate in this development, thus increasing the absolute amount of licensing fees they secure. Firms are likely to increasingly tap into this source, encouraging a continuous learning on the part of universities' technology transfer offices. Such development will spread 'best practices', as well as inducing new ways of carrying out business–university partnerships. This will be discussed in Chapters 6 and 7.

CHAPTER 4

Firms accessing university research results via spin-outs

In addition to collaborative/contract research and patent-based licensing, discussed in the previous chapters, spinning out a start-up company constitutes the third major vehicle for firms to capture university R&D/innovation. This process involves a particularly complex path for transferring technology, for two reasons: creating and growing a start-up is a daunting process in any case, and the university world is not generally well equipped to carry it out. Expertise in the business environment must be provided to complement the university contribution, as will be discussed in this chapter.

Firms capture the university knowledge and technology, by either partnering with the university spin-out company, or investing in it. Pharmaceutical companies, in particular, frequently buy equity in science-based university start-ups, while defining milestones along the downstream development of the product in question.

Example of a university spin-out

A university spin-out company is defined as a start-up that has concluded a licensing agreement with that university. In this way, the connection with the university is clearly established. In many instances, statistics list as spin-out companies any start-up established in the university science park, whether or not they have anything to do with the university.

Moving a new business idea or a technical innovation into a thriving commercial venture is an enormously challenging process, which requires vast amounts of energy, high resilience, and rapid learning, as well as numerous relevant business contacts. Let us look at one case in the life sciences.

The start-up NovImmune was created in 1998 in Geneva. It is based on research work carried out at the University of Geneva on retrovirus. In 1999, the start-up secured an exclusive license from the university in this area. This allowed the firm to launch its activity. At that time, the university decided to retain a small amount of equity in the firm. Later, NovImmune's work moved on to monoclonal antibodies. It now has several therapeutic products in this field. Close to 40 patents are protecting the company's position. The antibodies are produced within the company, which currently has 75 staff. Many activities are carried out outside and the firm is connected with close to 300 individuals outside the firm.

As the activity of the firm moved away from the scope of its initial license, the university would not have received anything, if it had negotiated only royalties and success fees in the initial deal. Since it elected to take equity in the start-up, it now benefits from the current success of the firm. In May 2009, the firm completed a fourth round of investment of CHF 62.5 million. Part of the company's contribution is a way to produce and select monoclonal antibodies. This generic technique does not include any proprietary know how and will soon be licensed out. In the near future, NovImmune may be ready for an initial public offering (IPO) on the Zurich stock exchange, which has developed a specialty in listing life-science companies.

The incubation process

The early phase of the transformation of a research project into a business is often called incubation. The term evokes the fragile period at the beginning of life. It is thought that the term comes from the Industrial Center real estate development in Batavia, New York. Back in 1959, in this small town in the north of New York State, the Mancuso family bought the vacated buildings of a Massey Harris plant for the fabrication of farm machinery. Not finding a large tenant to use the vast buildings, Joseph Mancuso decided to let to a number of local small companies, which needed an understanding landlord, in order to grow their business. The tenants were a wide variety of businesses, from manufacturing to service companies. They were not the young techno-ventures, which are the typical occupants of what we call incubators today. One of the first tenants was a chicken company, which prompted the name, conveying the idea of a nurturing place. However, this region did not become the US hotbed of innovation and entrepreneurship. Instead, the Boston area and Silicon Valley did, partly because of their access to institutions for higher education.

The steps encountered in incubating a techno-venture are illustrated in Figure 2. In this figure, the innovation projects draw from a pool of projects, which may be a university, or the R&D laboratories of a company, as was the case, for example, for the corporate British Telecom incubator Brightstar, in Ipswich, UK, in 2000. At that time, numerous corporate or independent incubators blossomed everywhere, close to 100 in the UK alone. In large part, the fashion for corporate venturing and incubators was riding on the exuberant dotcom wave, discussed in the following section. Let us look at the trajectory of one typical new venture, working hard to make its offering a success in the marketplace.

At the origin of the techno-venture is a technical idea and the first thing to do is to verify whether this idea is a practical one: the feasibility, or proof of concept, has to be validated as a first step

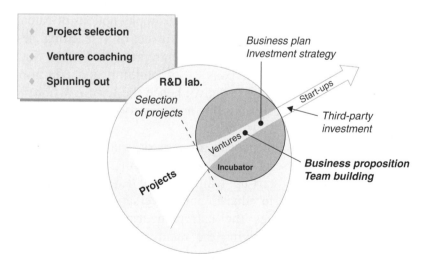

Figure 2 The incubation process for a technical venture

in the development project. If this first filter checks out positively, the development project may continue. Early on, the technical project must be folded into a technology-intensive business idea. This means that the technical innovative element is a tool in the hands of the entrepreneurs, for them to achieve success in the marketplace, whether it is a business-to-business situation (e.g., selling medical devices to hospitals) or a consumer market (e.g., electronic games). Too often, the entrepreneurs utter statements, such as: 'Our technology is so good, it will sell itself and we have no competition.' There is no such situation! Therefore, there is the need for an 'external' person to inject common business sense into the entrepreneurial team and ask the difficult questions on the business offering and the way to create value.

The business idea must be defined in terms of what it distinctly offers to clients, at what projected price and in what competitive environment. These issues require extensive, robust conversations, within the entrepreneurial team, but also with a variety of external persons, who bring knowledge and fresh questioning on the plan proposed to grow the business. For this, it is very helpful to have an experienced 'coach' following the venture, providing business information, managerial advice and asking hard questions of the entrepreneurial team. Depending on the topics – strategy, pricing, service offering attached to the product, patenting – the coach provides inputs and/or looks for the appropriate people to provide the information sought. At some point, for example, notions of patenting or market segmentation may be the object of a 'teaching' session when it best fits the need of the entrepreneurial team. Such *venture coaching* therefore consists of building and educating the team in a consulting perspective; hence the term *EduConsult* (IMD, 1999), which designates this non-classroom form of ad hoc executive education.

In all these steps, the coach, or mentor, and other external advisors are very useful to the venture team in several ways. Assumptions of the start-up team can be tested and business knowledge sharpened in educational conversations 'on-demand'. The coach accompanies the entrepreneurial team, but asks demanding questions, moving the team away from the often-encountered mindset of 'our start-up has no competitors'. The coach also alerts the team when they need to complement their range of skills, helping identify the appropriate new person who should join the team. Furthermore, the coach helps identify investors and prepare the team for raising funds.

If the venture reaches a stage at which it appears to be viable, investors are sought. Most ventures receive money from family and friends or 'business angels' – rich individuals. Even in the USA, where the venture capital (VC) industry is highly developed, less than 10 per cent of new ventures receive funds from institutional investors, such as a venture capital firms. In this case, a business plan is prepared to help convince the investors. The plan is a useful exercise to focus the minds of the entrepreneurial team, but it is valid only for a short time, since much of its contents will not be implemented, as a result of new information emerging and changes in the business environment. The business plan is thus very much a 'work in progress'.

The business plan is the usual tool through which a venture team engages with a venture capital firm. The first approach to an investor by the start-up should be by somebody with appropriate experience – the coach of the venture, for example. The reason is that venture capitalists (VCs) receive hundreds of business plans every year and they need advice and guidance as to which ones should retain their attention.

In a subsequent step, the entrepreneurial team may be invited to make a 'pitch' to a VC. It is important to prepare and rehearse such a presentation. The business case must be compelling, with attractive growth possibilities and financial prospects. The presentation must be made with clarity, concision and passion. Hence the cliché of the elevator pitch, often used in Silicon Valley: the entrepreneur must be able to clearly articulate to the listener the arguments to support the value of his/her business proposition during the time it takes to ride an elevator – a couple of minutes.

The venture capital industry represented investments of the order of $21 billion in the USA, in 2009. It suffered enormously from the credit crunch and from the financial crisis, which began in 2008. In such times, investors are very cautious and the depressed stock prices make an introduction to the stock exchange via the IPO route unlikely. Then trade sale, that is, selling the venture to a company, may be preferred. In the better times, however, VC is not a hugely profitable industry. It is very much a numbers game: one needs to invest in many ventures, in order to have a chance to have a start-up attain a real commercial and financial success. Thus the VC industry needs a large 'deal flow' of opportunities.

In this industry, a large return on investment is often described using the unfortunate war metaphor of 'blockbuster', which was a term applied to a bomb able to destroy a city block during World War II. Many successful companies, in fact, have never made use of VC money, but relied on private investments from family, friends and 'business angels'. The VC industry has a powerful public relations lobby and hammers home the message that it is a key engine of the US economy. More crucial is the entrepreneurial attitude of many people in the USA: they find sources of financing, VC industry or not.

One crucial element for the success of a VC firm is indeed the judgment of the 'partners'. The judgment is regarding the business potential of the project, but also, crucially, about the strength of the entrepreneurial team. Another key is the size and quality of the so-called 'deal flow', that is, the number of ventures and business plans to which the VC firm is exposed each year. This is a serious limitation for universities incubating their own start-ups: even if the university is very large, it is unlikely to generate a large number of potentially attractive ventures each year.

On average, the survival rate of start-ups is 25–30 per cent after five years. This low success rate is normal, resulting from the risks and difficulties for new ventures. This rate is similar all over the world, including in the famous Silicon Valley. Attempts to improve this survival rate include involving the entrepreneurial team of the start-up in an incubator, as discussed below.

The role of incubators

In incubators, the crucial part is certainly not the real estate – office, laboratories or pilot plant, which constitute commodities. It is not the shared secretarial services and fax machine either. What is crucial in an incubator is for the entrepreneurial teams to have access to relevant business knowledge and experience and to be relentlessly questioned 'for the good of the venture'. The 'venture coaching' described above aims to provide just that.

Too often, incubators provide the building and not the real value-adding 'software', such as relevant business knowledge. The juxtaposition of various entrepreneurial teams in the same incubator is thought to be enough for them to learn from each other. Indeed, this proximity is helpful, but competently 'facilitating' the learning process and the exchanges, as well as effective coaching, are enormously helpful. In the Brightstar incubator, in the Adastral Park in Ipswich, mentioned in the previous section, British Telecom had responsibly provided for a number of coaches to accompany the teams in their transition from being engineers to entrepreneurs.

In Cambridge, UK, the first incubator, the St John's College Innovation Centre, was founded in 1987 by St John's College, which is part of the University of Cambridge. This took place four years after the first European incubator was founded in Berlin in 1983. The St John Innovation Centre currently houses close to 70 start-ups. A key element of its success is that it fully supports and understands the specific needs of start-ups. For example, real-estate leases can be modified very flexibly to accommodate the fast-changing needs for space of a start-up, as it retrenches or expands. Also, there is a range of advisory services and events available, tailored to the needs of start-ups. The Innovation Centre receives financial help from non-profit organizations or public institutions, such as the Greater Cambridge Partnership.

Israel is characterized by a high entrepreneurial spirit, as well as by a general population that has a high esteem for education in general, and science and technology, in particular. To make use of this winning combination, compounded by a large number of technically educated immigrants in the 1990s, the Israeli government helped set up a chain of incubators to foster spin-out companies. Most of these were located in the proximity of a university, such as Technion, or a large laboratory, such as the Weizmann Institute. The latter, founded in 1934, now has more than 2,500 researchers, south of Tel Aviv (see www.weizmann.ac.il). As a result, a number of companies have emerged, in Israel, especially in the medical sector.[1] One of them is Teva, a world leader in the area of generic drugs.

Who starts techno-ventures? Engineers, of course. In transitioning from an initial technical concept to a business, the path is full of pitfalls; typically it is initially trodden by a small team of two or three persons, who know and trust each other, while combining the range of skills and orientations required to manage this formative period. In fact, the initial nucleus is often a duo of two friends, one more technically oriented and more 'introverted', the other more of an 'extrovert' and market-oriented. This was the situation in the founding of Sony, described below.

At the end of World War II, the start-up Sony emerged from the rubble of bombed Tokyo as a duo composed of the engineer, Mr Ibuka and the extrovert marketing man, Mr Morita. In the 1950s, this team had the vision that the recently discovered transistor would make it possible to produce pocket-sized radio sets. Therefore, they obtained the license for this application, from the inventor Bell Laboratories, where Bardeen, Shockley (who went to Palo Alto to be one of the pioneers of present day 'Silicon Valley') and Brattain, in 1948, had made this breakthrough invention, for which they received the Nobel Prize in 1956. In this case, Sony obtained the license for a very low prize to develop and manufacture pocket radio sets, which, in those days, were called 'transistors'.

At Bell Laboratories the invention of the transistor led not only to many new ventures, such as Sony; it was also truly at the origin of the remarkable, historical development of a whole new industry – that of the Information and Communication Technologies. Within such broad developments, the merits of individual new ventures, however, must be assessed with cool lucidity, as they often are obscured by hype, as discussed below.

The extravagant bubble of the dotcom start-ups

The case of the dotcom craze helps focus on some of the characteristics – highly financial, but also psychological – of start-ups. On occasion, the obsession with a lucrative 'idea to cash' process may create extreme 'boom and bust' cycles.

In the late 1990s, the world was very 'excited' by the so-called 'new economy'. At the time, media and politicians, especially in the USA, were broadcasting heroic messages about a new prosperity enabled by activities and innovations based on the internet and software, blessed with brand new business models. Banks and investors were driving this exuberant feeling. This was for a simple reason. The start-ups in this 'new economy', whether they originated from a university idea or elsewhere, were based on a business plan that could be implemented in very short time, since the internet was the vehicle. The dotcom business was a far cry from the situation where years are required to develop and qualify a new composite material for a civilian aircraft, for example.

At the height of the dotcom frenzy, it could thus take as little as 18 months for companies to go from the business idea to the first introduction on the stock exchange, which is the IPO. This meant that the investors, such as venture capitalists, quickly had a handsome return on their investment in the start-up. Another group of actors was doing well in this rapid 'idea to IPO' process: the financial institutions, which were 'advising' the start-up on going public. This included counseling the management, helping prepare the documents required by the stock exchange's regulatory authorities, organizing the appropriately named 'road-shows' to convince investors. Close to the IPO day, the financial institution would talk to colleagues in its network, in order to convince them to buy shares in the start-up, so that the IPO went well. For these services, the financial institution charged a fee that represented a fraction of the *value* of the firm at IPO. Such institutions had then, and, in fact, still have now, a huge incentive to push for IPO and to inflate the valuation of the start-up.

Some of these start-ups were launched by former students from Stanford University, which in the past had created the company SUN, standing for Stanford University Network. In these days of dotcom exuberance, a powerful example of the *herd effect* was at work, driven by the greed of some of the actors and the naive enthusiasm of many others. Values of firms were not assessed by looking at their potential, but by analogy with similar firms, having themselves been valued at inflated levels. This could not last forever and, in 2000, what was termed 'the biggest legal money-making process in history' became a huge wealth-destroying machine, taking all the stocks down. More than $5 trillion of market value was lost in the USA between the peak of March 2000 and late 2002. At that time, the composite index of the 'technology' companies, NASDAQ (which stands for National

Association of Securities Dealers Automated Quotations, www. nasdaq.com), had fallen to the level of 1994.

Companies such as Vivendi, which had seen the dotcom economy as a golden opportunity, were deeply shaken. Some of the issues involved are still in front of the US courts. Others, like Cisco or eBay, eventually flourished. In order to come out of this recession, US interest rates were kept low for several years, discouraging saving and encouraging consumption, ultimately resulting in another massive bubble, which burst in 2008 to produce the 'once in a century' economic crisis, which, for the first time ever, brutally and rapidly affected the *totality* of our highly interdependent world. Now we are waiting for the next, monetary, bubble, which may be even more devastating, for individuals and firms alike.

Lessons to learn from this extravagant episode include the fact that the value of a start-up is a fairly volatile and unscientific matter. If the area where the start-up is active is fashionable – fuel cells a few years ago, solar and wind energy technologies these days, for example – valuations of start-ups in that area are high … and the converse is true. Much 'valuation work' basically looks at what the market has been ready to pay for a similar company in the recent past. Furthermore, in periods of financial crisis, such as the 2008–10 period, going public (i.e., for an IPO) is highly problematical, so that, as mentioned earlier, selling the start-up to a company ('trade sale') becomes the back-up recourse, although it is likely to bring a lower return.

Another lesson concerns incubators themselves. At the time of the dotcom extravaganza, numerous incubators appeared – close to 100 in the UK alone within three years. The prevailing type was the self-funding model: the incubator provides services to the start-up in exchange for equity (shares) in that company. When the bubble burst, so did all these incubators.

Beyond the lessons of this grotesque crisis, it appears that incubators, anywhere in the world, cannot survive over the long run without some kind of public support or foundation money. It does seem that incubators should be considered as a public good and as an investment for the future. We now turn to a specific example of an incubator backed by a large higher education institution.

From science to business at Imperial Innovations

The Science and Technology Institute of Imperial College, in London, has 12,000 full-time students (one-third of them are graduate students) and 1,200 academic staff. It was founded in 1907. It was established in 1986 as a technology-transfer department, which became Imperial Innovations as a separate business in 1997. In 2006, this unit did an IPO and was thus introduced to the stock exchange Alternative Investment Market (AIM), raising £26 million (www.imperialinnovations.co.uk) in the process.

Imperial Innovations Group plc has 30 employees. It scouts for new ideas within the staff of Imperial College. In 2008, it filed 55 patent applications. It has seed money (including a grant of the order of £25,000) to help shape new ideas. In 2008, 11 new technology businesses were formed, bringing to 89 the total number of start-ups in the portfolio. It focuses broadly on start-ups active in three areas: energy, environment and health.

This model is unique in two ways. First, it is a public company listed on the London Stock Exchange. Second, it concentrates on making returns over investments with start-ups over the long term. The source of the innovations is the laboratories of Imperial College. As a sign of the times, the outfit has recently opened a subsidiary in India, together with a number of investors, including the Tata group. It will be interesting to see how this 'window on entrepreneurship' in India develops.

On average, there are 15 to 20 companies in incubation. This involves the activities mentioned above, as well as looking, at the appropriate time, for co-investors and senior management. In 2008, Imperial Innovations recruited 14 chairmen and 11 CEOs into their technology businesses. This ability of an institution like Imperial to attract 'big names' to lead their incubated companies, constitutes a considerable asset in our 'world of brands'. Such CEOs not only presumably know the business, but also have great business contacts, without which an entrepreneur has difficulty turning his/her venture into a commercial success.

At Imperial College Innovations, the current model generates revenues also from licensing income, of the order of £2 million per year. However, the focus is on spinning out start-ups and the unit seems to be aiming at increasing the 'deal flow', in order to be able to incubate roughly 15 new ventures per year. Given the volatility mentioned in the previous section, this may look a high-risk (high-return?) proposition, but the ventures in question are not the flaky internet start-ups of the Silicon Valley, vintage late 1990s. They are in areas where solid science and technology remain a key asset. These include medical devices and pharmaceuticals.

In the field of technology transfer from universities to firms, there is no single model that would fit all situations. Maybe there will never be one. The appropriate technology transfer vehicle depends on many factors: the nature of the innovation, the industrial sector considered, the local 'way of doing things', timing, etc. In any case, the evolution of the unique formula of Imperial Innovations should be followed with attention. Let us now look at how firms may benefit from universities' non-technical innovations and ventures.

Incubating non-technical ventures

In the previous section, we have discussed ventures which had a technical content.

It is usually assumed that incubators mainly concern technology-intensive start-ups. However, the very same principles of coaching and prototyping could be applied to ideas or ventures having nothing to do with technology. For example, one could envisage projects aimed at enhancing the customer experience when using cellular phones, although this kind of exploration is typically done by the handset manufacturers and operators themselves, using focus groups.

Firms could do a much better job of tapping into the universities' research in the social sciences to capture new ideas on customer experience, marketing, management practices, etc. Returning to the issue of self-service, the simple basic idea of IKEA's business model – buying low-quality furniture in kit – could well have been suggested by an innovative university sociologist, observing that products such as radio sets were sold as kits of parts to consumers for self-assembly by the US company Heathkit in the 1950s. Many innovations appear from adapting to one sector what is being done in another. This process could be more systematic by using an incubation approach.

New ventures in the area of business practices

Another possibility is to have experts from various horizons, including universities, working closely together. Productive areas could include designing new financial products ... hopefully more robust than the infamous and appropriately named 'subprime' loans. The closest thing to incubating non-technical ventures is in the service sector. Incubators sometimes host a small set of companies trying to develop a new service offering, usually using the internet. Since the end of the dotcom wave, discussed in the previous section, however, incubators rarely host services ventures.

This is unfortunate because, in order to generate cash, companies need a robust business model, new distribution concepts, or ways to improve customers' experience. These innovations are as effective and as necessary, as 'new' products. It seems that, in the non-technical areas, innovations happen haphazardly and are often an imitation of a competing offering. In this area, there is no protection of intellectual property, so that copying offers a rich vein by which the firm can find new offerings. The discipline of a well-developed incubation process would step up innovativeness in this area. Once the novel offering is identified and formulated it can be tested in the protected environment of an incubating unit, in order to detect the flaws and areas for improvements before implementation and launch.

Incubating a non-technical venture may thus be imagined as follows: let us take the example of a new ICT-enabled service, which a company wants to launch. A team of university academics (anthropologists, sociologists, etc.), well prepared to work together with managers of the company meet in disciplined, 'brainstorming sessions' to generate new concepts for business ideas. In a second step, these suggestions are evaluated and enriched/improved, in order to arrive at a short-list of potentially attractive ventures. These are then tested in 'prototypes', improved and assessed. If positive, the new concept is implemented.

We thus have a sequence very similar to the innovation process of a technology-intensive business idea. This is: *idea generation – evaluating – prototyping – iterating – testing in real life – implementing.* Firms should tap this mode of collaborative innovation more and more, as commercial success increasingly depends upon conceptual innovation, as well as innovative business models, backed with a good product, of course, and new approaches to doing business, such as open innovation or distributed innovation.

One such non-technical breakthrough was the 'self-service' approach in stores. This revolutionized the retail sector. It now has been standard practice for a long time. It appeared in specific instances, such as the Migros trucks serving as grocery stores in the Swiss countryside in the 1930s. It was only in the 1950s that the practice took off and stores rearranged their premises to proudly describe themselves as 'self-service', regardless of what they sold. The concept went on to be used elsewhere in various other retail outlets. The logic was the same: get the customer to do the work of picking up the goods and, indeed, assembling them, such as in the case of IKEA.

Metaventures to 'save the planet'

Enlarging the horizon, our world is facing a number of global challenges – climate change, water, food, energy, pandemics, demographic trends, reducing healthcare costs, while providing equivalent or improved quality in prevention and treatments. In particular, rising to the specific challenge of increasingly ageing populations requires a bold, innovative approach – which demands a much more comprehensive reappraisal than sector-specific, ad hoc solutions.

The knowledge available in universities could be much better used to help address, with novel concepts or with specific approaches, the large issues of the time, thus providing positive change towards a more sustainable world. This is a tall order, but leadership and political will, not money or technology, are the limiting factors. In particular, conceptual innovation is crucial, utilizing new ways to approach an issue. A university, or a group of universities, could, for example, design a fully comprehensive way of keeping ageing patients at home and treating them, in a reliable way, from a distance, using ICTs. Denmark is probably one of the countries which have pushed this logic the furthest. We are seriously limited by a conformist world, which muddles through, concentrating on fixing 'nuts and bolts' problems.

Such 'metaventures', putting together private companies and universities or public laboratories in large, ambitious projects, however, require that academics from various horizons accept the principle of effectively working together with firms. Indeed, as much as business ventures, such metaventures for the 'common good' demand *proper management, resources and motivation.*

At the level of specific industrial sectors, enterprises have much to offer in developing non-carbon energy sources, saving energy and building structures requiring no air conditioning and little heating. These growing activities have the potential to create massive number of jobs and this opportunity should be seized to the fullest. Indeed, tapping into university's expertise in an effective way is part of this process. At the time of writing, in 2010, however, China and Germany seem most serious about harnessing this momentum, for the good of the planet, but also to create jobs. Chapter 2 mentioned the new initiatives of the European Commission, Strategic Energy Technology, as well as the EIT. These are heading in the right direction, but much more needs to be done.

How effective is the spinning out from universities?

To show the effectiveness of the process of spinning out as a tool for wealth- and job-creation, rather than the number of start-ups per se, it is more important that these companies rapidly grow their number of employees and turnover.

In the complex process of spinning out start-ups, the quality of the entrepreneurial team is the first requirement to have a chance of success. Universities may not have the most business-savvy entrepreneurs available, either among the staff or their students. When looking at the environment of the 'incubated' start-up, two factors are paramount: good understanding of the business and good knowledge of markets. These two requirements for commercial validation of an idea are typically not fulfilled in universities. This results from the simple fact that the university world is focused on education and research, which are generally distinct from the universe of business, markets and competition.

From the above, it follows that the spin-out process should be envisaged by universities as second-priority vehicle for going from science to cash. If the university does want to go ahead with this vehicle, then it makes sense to do it with the help of an experienced partner, who is much closer to the realities of the market.

Examples of university-owned units for commercializing technology include those at the two leading British universities, Cambridge and Oxford, which have their own units: Cambridge Enterprise and Isis Innovation respectively.

Cambridge Enterprise was created on December 1, 2006 as a wholly owned subsidiary of the University of Cambridge. It provides a broad range of services: consultancy, technology transfer and seed fund/venture services. Its motto is: 'Commercialising University Science' (www.enterprise.cam.ac.uk). In its annual review (2007–8), the performance is assessed as follows: 116 invention disclosures, 83 patent applications, equity in 68 start-ups, and £8.8 million from consulting and licensing, excluding equity realizations. Of this sum, 82 per cent went to academics and to the university departments. The principles of Cambridge Enterprise are as follows:

(1) Accept into the portfolio those cases that have the strongest potential to make a significant positive impact.
(2) Take the course of action that supports commercialization of technology and work creativity to add value (or de-risk) the technology through the use of patent, proof of concept and evaluation and assessment resources.
(3) Work effectively with the inventor(s) to support their aspirations, manage conflicts and encourage synergy with the mission of the university.
(4) Find the best partner (licensee or start-up senior management and investors) to take the idea forward.
(5) Negotiate fair and reasonable terms that reflect the contribution of the assets and the expertise being transferred.

(6) Negotiate and close the greatest number of the best possible deals.

(7) Look after the deals once they are closed to encourage commercialization and optimize returns.

On the other hand, Isis Innovation was founded in 1988 as a wholly subsidiary company of the University of Oxford. The 2009 annual report of Isis (www.isis-innovation.com) mentions the following elements: 222 invention disclosures, 64 patents applications, four spin-out companies launched (OrganOx, Intelligent Sustainable Energy, Oxford Emergent Tuberculosis Consortium and Oxford Financial Computing) and total turnover of £5.6 million. Isis was created with the help of Professor Graham Richards, who recently retired as the head of chemistry department at Oxford. With close to 100 faculty members, this is one of the world's largest chemistry departments. It has a good track record in creating successful spin-out companies. In his recent book,[2] Richards extensively used the example of Oxford Molecular, a company he co-founded in 1989. The firm was floated in 1994, to be liquidated three years later.

To step up the spinning-out process, Oxford chemistry department struck a deal with the firm IP2IPO. This company made a down payment which allowed the department to erect a new building, in exchange for obtaining the equity of all spin-out companies emanating from the department. The financial firm also provided support and business advice to the start-ups.

Role of business schools

It is surprising to see how little business schools are involved in the incubation and development of start-ups. Incubators provide live 'case studies' and excellent opportunities for faculty members to practice their craft, while being directly useful to the entrepreneurial teams. It is as though they are primarily interested in strategy and marketing in large companies, or lucrative 'consulting' interventions in corporations.

If the business schools of universities, like the Imperial College's Business School, Oxford's Said Business School, or Cambridge's

Judge Institute, would channel more of their relevant expertise to the technology commercializing units, this could add a welcome contribution to accelerate and improve the success rate of the complex incubation process, and knowledge and technology transfer in general.

Usually, teams of MBA candidates are involved in projects dealing with commercializing of technology in the KTT office and, occasionally working to advise start-ups. Business schools in the USA are generally more active in this kind of 'advisory' role, but even there much more could be done.

As the world needs to make a serious effort to further job-creation and to move towards a more sustainable system, there would be scope for bold initiatives combining large engineering schools, business schools and the relevant value-creating firms. Such alliances would act as powerful accelerators for creating new activity and jobs.

The overall scene in the UK

The above section has used many examples from the UK, and the new process for evaluating universities, the Research Excellence Framework, is described in Chapter 6. The UK has, indeed, invested considerable efforts to promote university technology transfer, including the creation of start-up companies spun out of universities. A recent report by the British Venture Capital Association takes an overview of the recent evolution.[3] Since 2000, more than 40 technology-transfer offices have been established and 435 spin-out companies have been created by 36 UK universities.

Among OECD countries, the UK government is probably the one that is the most constantly concerned about the science-to-cash process. This is partly because many good universities are located in that country. Also, much talent and many ideas leave the country for other opportunities; hence the need to retain the wealth-creation process within the country. This is illustrated in a recent report by the UK Department for Business, Innovation and Skills.[4] This report stresses that firms must tap the resources available in universities more effectively, and universities should become more flexible in providing for business demands.

The UK is one of the countries most attentive to fostering innovation and entrepreneurship in universities, as they partner with firms. One of the places to discuss these issues is the National Council of Entrepreneurial Tech Transfer (NCET2). According to its website (www.ncet2.org), this organization brings together informal groups of universities in the UK seeking to bring entrepreneurs and investors' private equity (i.e., young firms not listed in the stock exchange) into the economy through involvement in the creation and funding of tech-transfer start-ups from universities.

For this organization, the term 'entrepreneurial tech transfer' is used to highlight the focus on entrepreneur recruitment, start-up creation, and funding, in contrast to traditional technology transfer, which generally relies on licensing patents to more established companies as a means to commercialize university and public laboratories. The aim of NCET2 is to provide a forum all stakeholders involved in the value-creation process.

The Peter Pan complex of Europe's young companies

There is considerable contrast between the USA and Europe in what becomes of young companies. In the USA, in recent decades, companies were born and became world champions: Microsoft, eBay, Google, Oracle, the renaissance of Apple, and so on. The list is impressive; the companies are largely concerned with ICT.

Where are the European counterparts to these success stories? They are few and far between. We could mention Nokia and Sony Ericsson in the mobile telephone business, partly because of the success of the GSM standards. There is also SAP. But the examples are scarce for such a powerful economic area. In the area of services, some newcomers have reached a global stature in the recent decades: ISS, from Denmark, for cleaning and facility management, and Club Med, but these successes cannot be found among technological firms. It is difficult to find reliable numbers without the 'hype' surrounding such issues. It is, however, probable that, in the recent decades, a successful start-up in the USA has generated in the order of five to ten more jobs than an equivalent company in Europe. Some may ask: how durable are these jobs? Is this so critical? Long-defunct computer pioneer Digital created, then destroyed many jobs, but laid-off employees went on to other firms and activities.

There is a complex set of reasons for this contrast between the two sides of the Atlantic. The fragmented European market, with the richness of diversity, mentioned earlier, comes with the cost of different legal and distribution systems, not to mention the language and cultural differences. Indeed, with its massive, fairly homogeneous market, the USA offers a field where the 'cost to grow' is much smaller for a young company. In this case, the European start-ups must integrate these impediments and innovate at a level and in a way that overcomes them. The key is to leverage this richness of diversity of varied cultures and different sophisticated markets, in order to turn them into an advantage. In many ways, Europe, by this diversity, is best equipped with the ingredients to succeed brilliantly in our cosmopolitan world. The key is to positively use these ingredients for success. Leadership and political will are two basic requirements for this.

There are other reasons, however, to explain this situation. One of them is what one of the authors of this book have called the 'Peter Pan complex' of European entrepreneurs. It does seem the many European entrepreneurs indeed work very hard at growing their business, with as much talent as anywhere else. However, their drive to grow to such a size that they would dominate their field is much less pronounced than, say, in the USA or China. The often-mentioned example is the region of Cambridge, UK, which is a hotbed of talented technical entrepreneurship, but very few large companies are thriving in this environment. One possible exception is ARM, the chip-design firm.

One even hears occasionally talk of small technology companies as 'lifestyle firms', meaning that workers are there to contribute and to have an enjoyable life, rather than being devoured by the need to grow rapidly and the ambition of dominating the market. It is unlikely that this expression would fly in Silicon Valley. This said, entrepreneurial spirit is not improving in the USA, but gradually increasing in most European countries, including Switzerland, according to the general surveys of the Global Entrepreneurship Monitor (GEM) (www.gemconsortium.org).

Asia is putting a high priority on spinning out companies from universities. The efforts in this area are considerable, but few Asian universities have been successful yet in this complex process. One of the most advanced is the University of Tokyo, as discussed below.

Spin-outs at the University of Tokyo

The University of Tokyo, often called 'Todai', is the most prestigious university in Japan. Like most of Japan's best universities, it is a national institution attached to MEXT, the Ministry for Education. In April 2004, the government undertook landmark reform to give the national universities considerable autonomy. They became National University Corporations. At the same time, the part of their budget coming from the Ministry started to decrease by 1 per cent per year, each year into the foreseeable future. There has even been recent talk of stepping up the cut to 3 per cent per year.

Universities have been strongly encouraged to increase their technology-transfer activities significantly. In support of this, more than 30 technology licensing offices were founded, within or next to universities all over the country. These TLOs were usually included into the university on the occasion of the 2004 reform. In support of this, the ownership of intellectual property generated in the course of projects supported with taxpayers' money has been transferred to the university.

Todai was founded in 1877 as the first national university in Japan. It has a president and a board. In the latter, half of the members come from outside the university. Among the internal board members, none represents the students. Todai has a full-time faculty of 4,000 for 29,000 students, and about half of them are post-graduates. Roughly 30 per cent of the graduate students are women, while 25 per cent are not Japanese. The largest group (more than 2,000) of graduate students is in the Faculty of Engineering. It also has a large Faculty of Medicine. Todai, therefore, has a powerful pool from which to generate technical innovations. In fiscal year 2007–8, a total of 658 innovation disclosures were received, as compared with 450 for Stanford

University. The plans are for well over 650 such disclosures each year, as the 'deal flow' seems to steadily increase, paralleling the enhanced interest of faculty and students for knowledge and technology transfer.

In terms of contract research with industry, the current amount is $65 million. This compares favourably with the largest US universities doing research with firms. Industrial projects are relatively small, typically $50,000 to $100,000 per year, over several years. In November 2009, the first non-Japanese company started large-scale collaborative research at Todai. It is the Swiss food company Nestlé, which now has a small team in residence, contracting R&D out to Todai's nutrition group, as well as to other institutions in Japan.

On the other hand, royalty income from licensing was $1 million in 2008. It is generated with the help of the technology-transfer office (CASTI) (www.casti.co.jp). Several of the licenses are granted to the Todai start-ups, discussed below.

Launching start-ups is an important part of Todai's commercialization of technology. It currently has an $80 million fund (the fund is managed by the University of Tokyo Edge Capital (UTEC), a dedicated VC to the University of Tokyo) and started a new, $100 million fund in 2009. UTEC has invested in 34 Todai-related companies so far. In the years 2004–9, approximately 20 firms have been spun out, in the medical technology and life-sciences sectors, benefiting from the university's strong medical school, but also expertise in ICTs and materials sciences

By law, national universities cannot own university start-ups. However, the universities are allowed to receive equity in the new ventures, instead of royalty payments. The equity of the seven current start-ups is held by the university. Of them, it is expected that two or three will become public (IPO) or be successfully acquired within three years. One of UTEC portfolio companies, Tella Inc., which is a dendritic cell (DC) vaccine therapy company, went public on March 26, 2009. Its stock price at the time of the IPO was ¥ 300, and went as high as ¥ 1,500–2,000 in November 2009, at which time its market capitalization was approximately US$ 1.7–2.0 million.

China is also strongly emphasizing the role of universities in creating employment. Its government, at the federal and provincial levels, in particular, but also at the municipal level, has a dynamic policy of encouraging science parks, connected with universities, as described below.

Science parks in China

To western observers, China's physical positioning of science parks and incubators is somewhat counterintuitive. Contrary to the expectations of a campus-like environment, many science parks are urban and housed in tall office buildings. For example, the science park of the University of Tsinghua, in Bejing, occupies several floors of an office building, owned by the university. Most of the 'incubated' start-ups are in information technology, so that office space is appropriate. Life-sciences activities make use of the university's laboratories. The director of the science park has a staff of 15 persons scouting for attractive projects going on in the laboratories of the university. Seed money, of the order of $100,000 per firm, is available for the start-ups. A program of mentorship provides coaching to 20 young entrepreneurs each year. The latter may also make use of an extensive offer in courses and workshops.

Five years ago, the science park created a fund of €50 million, for early-stage and development financing. It is too early to have success stories yet, but, when these come, they are likely to be in the IT industry. In China, there are an estimated 25,000 firms currently working on offering services on the web or for mobile telephony. Most of these are concentrated in Beijing and Shanghai. Clearly, several of these will grow in the world's largest and most dynamic market for mobile telephony. Some may well be world leaders in their field.

Broadening further the concept of the science park, the Zhongguancun Science Park ('Z Park'), in Beijing, includes areas where there is a high concentration of educational and research institutions. This represents a huge area of 232 square kilometres (4 per cent of Beijing if you imagine surrounding the city in a 70km-sided square).

The umbrella organization of the Z Park was created by the Beijing municipality in 1988, to include ten 'sub parks', in which are 39 universities and 4 million students. A total of 20,000 companies, of all sizes, are active in this large area. The main role of this organization is in policy-making (reduced tax rate, educational programs, etc.), infrastructure and coordination among the various districts involved. A high priority at this stage is to foster international contacts. For example, the region has a connection with the similarly government-inspired Sophia Antipolis area, near Nice, in southern France, for various exchanges and collaborations.

The Z Park has a website to provide entrepreneurs with information on available business coaches, educational courses, and sources of funding. Statistics mention 5,000 start-ups within this catchment area. The question is, indeed: out of these, how many are really 'legitimate' start-ups, which will eventually hire staff, grow and flourish, truly creating employment?

A considerable asset for China consists in the large diaspora of students and professionals abroad. A substantial flow of these individuals is coming back to China, in order to seize the opportunities available in the country. These 'returnees' concentrate on the Beijing and Shanghai areas. They are younger than in the recent past, as students now often come back to China as soon as they have completed their studies abroad, in Japan, Europe or the USA. Seed money is available from government sources, specifically to help them start a company. As an example, in the Beijing science park of the Beihang University, 80 per cent of its 216 start ups are in the IT sector and 40 per cent of them are managed by returnees.

Competing with Beijing, the Shanghai area is also a world center for business: it is putting a particular emphasis on life sciences for its future development. Several science parks are dedicated to this field and the municipality has ambitious plans to make of Shanghai one of the world's centers in life sciences, biotech and medical technology. The Shanghai Jiang Biotech and Pharmaceutical Business Development claims to have China's largest concentration of pharmaceutical companies (seven out of the 12 largest in the world), with several research centers and more than 300 SMEs in this sector (www.zjbpb.com).

China's venture capital industry has considerably developed in the last decade. However, the involvement of government in these funds is excessive and the industry lacks a proper legal framework. These issues are gradually being addressed. This brings us to the country where venture capital was invented and effectively deployed: the USA, as discussed below.

From route 128 to Silicon Valley and Bangalore's Silicon plateau

In the 1960s, a number of graduates from the many universities and colleges in the Boston area started their own company. These included Digital, now defunct, and Thermoelectron, which span out companies, to be introduced to the stock exchange within an average of five to six years, as compared to more than ten years in Europe.

This movement of start-up creation was surfing on developments that had started well before this, when the concept of venture capital (VC) was invented by the Frenchman Georges Doriot, as he created American Research Development, in Boston in 1946. The venture capital dynamic is credited to be a major positive force, although a very small number of start-ups receive investments from them, as mentioned earlier. Seed money typically comes from family and friends, not-for-profit organizations, or rich individuals, sometimes called 'business angels'.

In the 1960s, many entrepreneurs located their start-up along Route 128 around Boston, as it was a convenient location with commercial premises at affordable prices. More or less at the same time, entrepreneurial spirit was finding another home in a small region south of San Francisco, around Palo Alto and the campus of Stanford University. Engaged in the creation of firms, which later became Intel, Hewlett-Packard, etc., supported by the knowledge available at Stanford University, this movement also benefited from the fairly massive amounts of taxpayers' money funding public laboratories and also NASA being in the region. What became known as Silicon Valley is now synonymous with entrepreneurial energy all over the world. Many people from outside the USA come to this hotbed of entrepreneurial spirit. In fact, about half of the entrepreneurs in Silicon Valley do not have an American passport. Many entrepreneurs originate from China, Taiwan and India.

In 2008, the USA have created a total of 595 start-ups, according to an AUTM report for 2008,[5] university-connected and otherwise. This is slightly higher than in previous years. This number does not seem high, compared with the 435 spin-out companies created by 36 universities in the UK, as reported earlier in this chapter. As a rough comparison, it is estimated that the European countries have created a total of 630 to 650 start-ups (ASTP estimate) in 2008.

Bangalore, India, chose a name, Silicon Plateau, inspired by California to depict its start-up activity. This region of India has many higher education institutions and one company, which has become the icon for its entrepreneurial spirit: Infosys.[6] As indicated in Chapter 1, this IT services company was founded in 1981 by seven computer engineers. Their vision for the company did not have much to do with revenues and profits, as they wanted to create the most respected company in India. For its customers, this company would deliver on promises and meet expectations. For its employees, it would create an open, fair meritocracy. For investors, it would provide consistent financial performance.

As of the end of 2010, Infosys counted more than 105,000 staff working in 22 countries, with sales in excess of $4 billion per annum; it has come a long way since its days as a start-up. Furthermore, Infosys' profitability is better than the average in this industry.

One of the reasons of the success of Infosys is, indeed, the quality of its management. It also the fact that it has kept the meritocratic, no-nonsense approach typical of start-ups. Any corporation should remember vividly that, once, it was a start-up.

Entrepreneurial Israel

Israel constitutes a remarkable example of interaction between entrepreneurs, technical innovation and investors. Most of the information below is taken from my 'Israel: A Powerhouse for Networked Entrepreneurship'.[7]

First, this country's population greatly values knowledge, science and technology. It has one of the world's highest percentages of scientists and engineers within its population. The country has notable institutions, such as the Weizmann Institute and the Technion. Israel is one of the countries in the world investing the most in R&D, close to 5 per cent of GDP per annum, that is, double the OECD average.

Second, the venture capital (VC) industry in Israel is comparable in size with that of a much larger country, such as the UK. Roughly, 60 per cent of these investments come from the USA. The model is thus for a start-up: innovation/R&D is located in Israel, investors and headquarters are in the USA – often Delaware for legal and tax reasons – providing access to the world's largest economy.

Israel has 24 technology incubators, of which 16 are privately owned. The model seems to work, particularly in the healthcare sector. In the area of medical devices, there are close to 200 companies in Israel, contributing substantial export revenues to the country. Another feature specific to the entrepreneurial scene in Israel is the Army. As a man joins the Army for a three-year period, he is likely to be 18 years old. In many cases, the Army encourages combining military service with academic studies in science and engineering. Special programs are set up for this. Furthermore, the Army entrusts the young person with responsible jobs, such as managing development projects on sophisticated technologies, with budgets of €1–2 million per annum. The soldier thus has acquired the following:

- considerable management experience in managing large, challenging projects;
- extensive network with colleagues, but also with firms involved in the project;
- mastery of a technical innovation.

After completion of military service, the ingredients are all there to start a company, and many persons do so. The Army is quite generous about transferring the technical innovation to the start-up, except for the most sensitive military uses. It is estimated that close to two-thirds of Israel's start-ups make use of some kind of Army-developed technology or experience.

As an example of the intensity of the technology transfer taking place in this country, let us note that, each year, the Weizmann Institute, mentioned above, receives $250 million in royalties. This figure is much higher than the best-performing licensing universities anywhere in the world.

Spin out or not spin out? this is the question

Some authors suggest that spinning out should take place as late as possible and is, in fact, as a last resort. They claim that it is often not such an effective way to make money out of a technology-intensive business.[8]

Keep the venture as a project

It may be argued that, in many cases, the start-up is incorporated into a company too early. Many start-ups actually constitute one development project, which takes time and considerable effort to metamorphose into a true commercial venture, if it ever attains this maturity. Incorporating companies prematurely sometimes results from the fact that entrepreneurs are anxious to drape themselves in the clothes of the glamorous CEO position, although it is often meaningless. What is the real glamour in being CEO of a two-person firm for four years, before it goes bankrupt?

Creating a company is expensive in that it induces considerable overheads. An incorporated firm, even very small, must have its own administrative arsenal, even if staff, such as the human resources or financial person, for example, are part time. It must have an advisory council to debate and guide the future of the firm. Thus, there is an argument for strictly screening projects and keeping some of them with the status of project within the university, which has the administrative capability to handle many projects. In the meantime, with appropriate seed money, the real business potential may be assessed, together with experienced outsiders, such as the coaches mentioned above. Rather than moving an activity to an incubator and incorporating the project into a start-up that will die in a few years, the activity would remain in the university department as an R&D project, providing worthwhile employment, financed by granting agencies or firms, but phased out when the prospects appear not promising enough.

Creating a spin-out company: a last resort?

The same authors[9] claim that many technologies are best exploited by licensing or sale rather than founding and growing a company. Accordingly, the technology should move as late as possible from the university to the incubator. The exploitation of the technology by means of creating a company should also take place as late as possible. Thus:

> Exploitation should not be done via company creation unless it can be clearly shown that this is the surest and best way to create value – and even then, events such as relocation and company formation should be done as late as possible, in order to contain costs, risks and expectations.

This clear-cut message assumes that the only mission of the university knowledge and technology transfer office is to create value, measured by money, for the parent university. This is debatable, since often the key mission is to disseminate knowledge into society. Furthermore, the principles above should be adapted to the particular circumstances, such as the nature of the innovation and the industrial sector, where it is expected to be deployed.

In brief, by keeping a watch on key incubators, university or university-linked incubators, firms secure a window on new developments, which may ultimately contribute to enhancing the health of ongoing businesses, trigger the creation of new ones, or even make parts of their businesses obsolete. At a minimum, this watching provides a source of information on what is happening outside the firm, as it monitors the development of the relevant ventures.

In some cases, it may be justified for the firm to invest (i.e., buy shares, or equity) in the start-up, or to acquire the whole start-up at the appropriate time. Pharmaceutical companies often do, in order to have access to new therapeutic solutions. The challenge is even more acute than when acquiring a new venture, as for Roche when it acquired Genentech: the buyer must be careful not to 'digest' the acquisition by incorporating it fully into its operations, as this would destroy the highly valuable entrepreneurial spirit of the young company, the staff of which precisely do not want to work in the much more bureaucratic environment of large firms. This would undoubtedly result in chasing the talent away from the venture, as entrepreneurs rarely thrive under the rules and culture too rigidly imposed by a corporate buyer. This illustrates one key difference between large corporations and SMEs, which is the topic of the following chapter.

CHAPTER 5

SMEs must engage with universities

The previous chapters have dealt with the three main types of partnership between universities and, generally, large firms, in an attempt to bridge the gap between science to business. Collaborations between universities and SMEs constitute a specific case. This is because such firms have significantly fewer resources available, in staff and money, than multinational corporations. These constraints make it a particular challenge for them to carry out any kind of R&D, including engaging with external partners for collaborative developments. These include the three vehicles discussed earlier: research and development, licenses, and spin-out firms, but particularly the first two.

In most countries, a large majority (typically 75 per cent) of manpower works in SMEs. Among these, the technology-intensive ones are often not in a competitive position in the long run, because they are not up to date either technically or in their business and management practices. More and more 'South–South' collaborations take place. Many countries attempt to encourage smaller companies to engage with universities, in order to enhance/protect their competitive position and benefit from having access to global markets. Fostering such partnerships may involve manpower, financial help and fiscal incentives, as discussed below.

SMEs and competitiveness

What is an SME? According to the European Union's definition, an SME is a firm which has fewer than 250 employees and a sales volume (turnover) below €50 million. In practically all countries, a large faction of the workforce is employed by such firms. By carrying out timely and appropriate developments, SMEs place themselves in a better position for leveraging global markets. This allows them to offer better value to customers and to commercialize more differentiated products. Also, this boosts their productivity. The resulting profitable growth creates jobs back home.

Conversely, in due course, the lack of technological and business 'updating' is bound to result in bankruptcy for many firms, in the USA, Europe, as well as Japan, as they will be unable to compete with the dynamic firms from 'emerging' economies. This structural problem is made much worse by the current, serious economic crisis, which started in 2008. The downturn of the economy and the credit crunch are very seriously hurting the world of SMEs. Most governments have put in place emergency measures to provide bridging loans, in order to help them pass this cash-tight, low order-book phase.

Enabling smaller firms to remain competitive is a relatively low-risk route towards creating employment, as compared with corporations, which reduce their workforce in the most industrialized countries, and the start-ups, which are seen as an exciting area, but have, on average, a 25 per cent survival rate after five years of existence. Therefore, it is somewhat surprising to see the 'benign neglect' of governments shown towards SMEs as a potential source of jobs.

To caricature somewhat, in the recent past, the most industrialized economies have aligned the 'framework conditions' (tax system, laws and regulations, etc.) of their business environment with what large corporations want, while making much noise about promoting start-ups, and being fairly ineffective at helping SMEs. This is in spite of the fact that, in all countries, roughly 75 per cent of the total labour force is employed in SMEs, as already mentioned. In the USA, for example, such firms represent a substantial engine for job-creation.

One could also argue that the international system has been designed for corporations and not small companies. One example is the practice of transfer pricing, which requires the existence of 'tax havens', such as Jersey, Caribbean islands, Panama, etc. This practice works as follows: a corporation sells its goods and services at a low price, to one of its subsidiaries, located in one of these so-called tax havens. This subsidiary sells them to another unit of the same company, with a high price, but the tax on the resulting profit is very low, since, by design, it occurs in a tax haven. The firm has thus maximized its profit at the location where the tax is lowest, allowing it to reduce, often by as much as 60 per cent, the amount of tax on corporate profits paid in its home country. This represents billions of euros that do not go to the national treasuries, much more than tax evasion by individual taxpayers. As one executive once quipped: 'a good tax-lawyer can do wonders for the profit and loss accounts of a corporation'. Transfer pricing is not practiced by SMEs, which thus pay their profit taxes in full in their home country.

Indeed, many smaller firms are active in the sectors of retail and handicraft, unlikely to engage with university R&D, although, as all human institutions, they could well make use of fresh ideas, such as modified business models and up-to-date managerial practices, or effective use of IT systems. In the OECD countries, a small fraction, 3–5 per cent, of SMEs operate in an innovation-intensive, technical environment. These benefit most from engaging with universities. This is particularly the case of the generally high-performing *Mittelstand* (meaning 'medium-sized' in German) companies in Germany. Such firms employ close to 70 per cent of the German labour force and routinely have contacts and collaborations with universities or public institutions. In Switzerland, out of the 300,000 SMEs existing in the country, it is estimated that 10,000 of them are in a position of interacting with universities. This proportion is in line with the percentage given above.

Around the world, attempts are made to sharpen the managerial and technological capabilities of SMEs, particularly by enabling them to benefit from relevant contributions of external partners, universities in particular. In this area, a first issue is the financing; a second one is the availability of staff. One model for overcoming these constraints is Small Business Innovation Research (SBIR), in the USA, discussed below.

SBIR in the USA

Small Business Innovation Research (www.sbir.gov) is one of the best-known programs for SMEs in the USA. It is presented as an efficient model to boost the competitiveness of small companies in many countries. It is funded by requesting federal agencies spending more than $100 million in extramural R&D activities to provide 2.5 per cent of their said budget for SBIR-related grants. In 2009, the SBIR budget was $2.9 billion. SBIR has a strong connection with universities. In a firm survey of SBIR recipients, more than one-third of the respondents reported some university involvement (university faculty, graduate students and/or technology) and two-thirds reported that, at least, one of the founders was an academic. About 27 per cent used university faculties as consultants and 17 per cent entered into research partnerships with universities.[1]

For the direct funding of R&D projects to SMEs, in addition to SBIR, there are two programs: the Small Business Technology Transfer (STTR) and the Advanced Technology Programs (ATP), which, each year, provide several billion dollars to SMEs, in order to stimulate technological innovation through additional R&D activity.

STTR is also funded by federal agencies that have to reserve a portion of their R&D budget for STTR-related grants. The STTR funds cooperative projects involving a small business and a research institution, where both partners must perform about the same percentage of the work. Specific non-exclusive background intellectual property access rights can be mutually provided by the partners. The company usually has the option to negotiate an exclusive royalty-bearing license on the IP generated during the execution of the project.

Both of the above schemes are structured in three phases (Phase I: Feasibility $100,000; Phase II: Development $750,000; Phase III: Commercialization).

They are presently under review for extension until 2023 by the US House and Senate. One criticism of SBIR is that the grants are constructed to be provided to the projects most likely to succeed and, hence, they simply allow the company to save the money it would have invested anyway in the project. Some studies demonstrate, however, that companies with SBIR grants create more jobs than others.[2]

The ATPs provide direct R&D funds to small companies, in order to bridge the gap between the research laboratory and the marketplace. All industries and all fields of science are eligible, as long the company contributes at least the indirect costs of the project. The main criteria are the technological needs of American industry and how the project can best benefit the nation. In contrast with the SBIR/STTR programs, the allocation of funds is driven by industry. A total of $140 million have been awarded in fiscal year 2007, about half of the budget available ten years earlier ($253 million in 1997[3]). The scheme is based on a bottom-up approach, that is, companies submit proposals. This system is sometimes criticised in that the peer review process to evaluate the proposals involves too many academics and therefore does not look sufficiently at the business potential of the projects.

Usually considered as successful initiatives, these programs improve the capacity of firms to absorb technologies from public research organizations (PROs), which are often at an early stage – that is, only research feasibility has been demonstrated. The commercial feasibility of the project remains to be proven. It also encourages firms to develop new technologies which are considered useful by the government.

When available, these schemes provide the best opportunity for an SME to engage in much more groundbreaking R&D than they would otherwise. They provide good incentives for companies to enhance their interest in the technologies and expertise in public laboratories. This is what is sometimes referred to as providing market traction.

Effectiveness of SBIR

As mentioned, outside the USA, SBIR administration is often viewed as a model. Inside the USA, there is a fair amount a debate about its real efficiency and effectiveness on economic innovation-led growth. As an example, let us take a recent US parliamentary evaluation.[4] In its report, Congress underlines a number of issues. First, the VC industry does not provide enough seed money, so the SBIR is fulfilling a useful role. Second, the budget available to the SBIR programs have increased in recent years. Third, the current legislation prohibits the use of SBIR and STTR funds to cover the program's administrative costs, including commercialization assistance, technical assistance beyond $4,000 per phase, program evaluation, and salaries. This is unfortunate, since such costs may be critical to the programs' effectiveness. Fourth, SBIR's support is attractive to entrepreneurs, because it consists of awards or grants and contracts. These do not dilute company ownership.

This assessment highlights insufficient seed funding available to firms for their development. A similar situation is deplored in most OECD countries. Generally, assessments of the SBIR make the point that the developments financed by this organization would not have taken place otherwise. Thus, the resulting commercial and social benefits are clearly to its credit.

Encouraging applied research in SMEs

Aside from the USA and its SBIR programs, many countries have made attempts to help SMEs fund R&D projects, carried out in collaboration, particularly with universities. These are discussed below, beginning with R&D tax credit schemes.

Tax incentives

Many countries have put in place fiscal deductions, aimed at promoting R&D investments by SMEs.

In the USA, the 2008 stimulus package, to alleviate the cataclysmic Wall Street-triggered crisis, retroactively granted a two-year extension to a credit which may yield a saving of up to 6 per cent in federal tax credit: to this should be added the credits granted by individual countries.

Often termed 'the most effective in Europe', a tax credit sheme was introduced in France in the 1980s by the then Minister of Research, Hubert Curien. It was strengthened in 2008. This tax credit is now volume-based. It is 30 per cent for the first €100 million euros, with a 50 per cent preferential rate for the first year, 40 per cent for the second year and 30 per cent for subsequent years. It thus strongly encourages a positive dynamics of an increase of R&D investments.

In the UK, 80 per cent of the 6,600 tax credit claims (representing £670 million) in 2008, came from SMEs. By and large, this meant that the R&D costs of these firms were reduced by 10 per cent.

In 2007, Italy introduced a tax credit scheme, by which up to 40 per cent of the cost is covered, if a university is involved. It consists of a 10 per cent flat credit for R&D investments. A higher rate of 15 per cent is applied to SMEs. This may help somewhat the present unsatisfactory situation, where Italy invests only half as much as the OECD average in R&D. It is particularly important to the many entrepreneurial SMEs of northern Italy. This gives them more incentives to collaborate with universities and the institutes of the Consiglio Nazionale delle Richerche (CNR), mentioned later in this chapter.

Singapore has a comprehensive set of measures to promote R&D activities in SMEs, as will be seen later in this chapter.

Funding

The issue of access to financing is described as critical by small companies in most countries. These firms generally find that banks do not want to task the risk to accompany them in their development projects. One way to mitigate this is for the government to help finance them.

One incentive is to fund the SME for a fraction of the cost of projects carried out with a partner. This is often done on a matching fund basis: the firm pays 50 per cent and a government grant covers the other half. In interacting with SMEs, the universities carrying out applied R&D with firms should be well aware of the sources for funding available, so that they can propose a project and the way to finance it at the same time.

The SME may also benefit from a low-interest loan, reimbursable only if the project leads to commercial success. One such example is Oséo, in France, dedicated to supporting innovation in small companies. *Oser* is the French word meaning 'to dare'. Headquartered near Paris, it has a decentralized action thanks to its 42 regional offices. Oséo results from the merger of the innovation agency ANVAR together with a bank for the development of SMEs and the Agency for Industrial Innovation (AII). In 2008, Oséo acted as an innovation advisor and provided loans to 5,000 SMEs, totalling €800 million. To counteract the 'crisis of the century', in 2008–9, part of the stimulus package was to allow Oséo to help the cash flow situation of 23,500 SMEs, accounting for up to 90 per cent of their loans, in 2009, representing a total of €6 billion.

Certain institutions have the specific mission of carrying out applied R&D for small firms. In a sense, they act as a conduit allowing university research to be transferred into knowledge in a form relevant for SMEs. One such organization is the Fraunhofer Society, mentioned in Chapter 3. Founded in 1949 in Bavaria, it takes its name from the Bavarian inventor-entrepreneur, Joseph Fraunhofer, who was active in the area of spectrometry and optics in the 19th century. By 2009, the society had 15,000 members of staff in 57 institutes, in more than 30 German locations, usually close to universities. Out of the total €1.4 billions of the Fraunhofer Society's revenue, 60 per cent comes from firms and 40 per cent comes from public funds. The latter makes it possible for the institutes to develop and maintain specific areas of expertise. Through this public 'subsidy' to the society, SMEs have access to university-produced research via the 'channel' constituted by the Fraunhofer institutes. Indeed, many Mittelstand companies make use of this channel for commercializing technology.

Equivalent to the Fraunhofer Society is the Dutch contract research organisation TNO, headquartered near Delft's technological university. With 4,300 professionals, this non-profit organization had a turnover of €579 million in 2007. Part of its focus is to collaborate with SMEs in the Netherlands.

In the UK, the government website www.businesslink.gov. uk offers no-nonsense help to SMEs 'to save time and money by giving instant access to clear, simple and trustworthy information'. It gives information on grants and incentives available for fostering SME–university collaborations. Such a program boosts innovation (www.smeinnovation.org), provides days of free consultancy/advice to the SME, followed, if need be, with a secondment of qualified personnel of up to three months, as well as providing possible grants of up to £30,000, in order to help the

SME develop new offerings or improve its business operations, largely by involving a local university.

In Japan, 70 per cent of all employed persons work in a SME. In spite of this, for many years, government policies seemed to be only concerned with the large companies, essentially ignoring the SMEs. This relative neglect went on until 1999, at which time the fundamentals of SME law were radically revised. This marked a significant change in policy, as it has come to be considered that these firms represent a vital part of the economy. Many SMEs in Japan have, however, disappeared since 1995 – causing a decrease in employment of 30 per cent, so it is questionable how successfully this change of point of view was put into practice.

A dedicated agency, part of METI (Ministry of Economy, Trade and Industry) provides managerial advice to SMEs. It was created in 1963 and its website is www.chusho.meti.go.jp. It is a pretty bland compilation of websites and publications. Another agency provides region-specific information: its website is www.sme.ne.jp. It gives hands-on information to the smaller firms present in the relevant prefecture (which is the name given to Japanese regions).

In the European Union, the Framework Programme, already mentioned, welcomes the participation of SMEs. Many of them take part in projects, obtaining useful windows on technology and markets in this way. However, since negotiating project proposals with the EU is very time-consuming, small companies do not make the time to participate in these negotiations. The latter are conducted either by academics or managers of corporations. When the project is close to being funded, then SMEs are invited to join in as appropriate, in order to contribute their specific know how and benefit from interacting and collaborating with the other members of the project, thus learning about partners, customers and future markets.

Adopted in June 2008, the Small Business Act for Europe (SBA) reflects the European Commission's will to recognize the role of SMEs in the EU economy and for the first time puts into place a framework for SME policy for the EU and its member states.[5] The Act aims at simplifying the legal and administrative environment in which SMEs operate. It proposes four legislative proposals to translate this objective into action. The aim is to create an environment, in which entrepreneurs thrive and entrepreneurship is rewarded. With an 'Erasmus for young entrepreneurs' program, entrepreneurs may take advantage of cross-border mobility, as well as gaining experience and insight by spending time in SMEs in different countries. Also, honest entrepreneurs who have faced bankruptcy should quickly be given a second chance, by promoting a positive attitude in society towards a fresh start. Changing bankrutpcy law in this way indeed constitutes a strong message to society in favor of entrepreneurship. Similarly, public procurement should favor SMEs' products and services. More funds will be available at the early stage.

Cost sharing

A third approach is for several SMEs to join forces in financing a common project. These 'multi-client' programs, or consortia, are a mechanism for sharing costs, as discussed earlier in Chapter 2. It may apply particularly well to firms that have a limited budget for innovation projects. Indeed, it is complex to 'align' different companies on a common work program and contractual details have to be carefully set up. Such an approach can even include patent and intellectual property rights. This requires that the rights of each participating company are clearly defined, by field of use and by geographical territory. This sorting out, in turn, demands considerable negotiations and management attention.

Pooling resources in this way applies to management training as well: each of a group of SMEs sends managers to participate in a joint course, so that a total of 25 to 35 participants can, as a group, follow a course specially organized for them. Examples of what is covered on such a course could be techniques of quality control, managing effective teams, etc. Such a formula allows sharing the cost, but also promotes contacts and dialogue among managers from various companies, which can be very beneficial later on.

In addition to funding R&D, another issue encountered by smaller firms is the lack of personnel available to carry out innovation projects. This limitation may be mitigated by different measures, discussed below.

Providing SMEs with external management expertise

Many national organizations are helping fund experts so that they can work for a period of time alongside the management of SMEs. Very often, 'young retirees' from large corporations provide this resource. Such efforts could be stepped up in many cases, as 'senior' managers, often organized in associations or listed on a website, are very motivated to pass their experience on to younger actors in a similar field and they are relatively free to travel and to live abroad for a few weeks at a time.

An example is the London-based European Bank for Reconstruction and Development (EBRD). Since 1991, this bank has invested close to €42 billion in 30 countries from central Europe to central Asia. Most projects have the goal of ushering in a more sustainable economy. For example, a large effort has been made to improve energy efficiency. In addition, in order to combat the disastrous financial crisis of 2008–10, it increased its financing by 55 per cent in 2009.

This bank is the single biggest investor in the region. The corresponding 2,500 funded projects so far include numerous SMEs. As a result, the bank runs an extensive program which funds experts to temporarily serve as advisers to these SMEs. They spend short-term periods at the company premises over a period of a few months. As with 'venture coaching', discussed in Chapter 4, such advisers act as a resource, providing advice, as well as relevant business contacts.

Another resource available as a method of providing temporary contributions to SMEs is graduate students. Several schemes exist to foster such collaborations between firms and post-graduates; several are presented below.

Encouraging university graduates to work with SMEs

Many initiatives aim at encouraging university researchers to work for SMEs. These indeed alleviate a key bottleneck in the SMEs' situation and may be more effective than providing grants. These programs are offered at the national or regional level. In some cases, these programs are transnational, such as those from the European Union.

At the regional level

In Belgium, regional governments finance projects presented by an SME and carried out by a graduate student in a local university. For example, the French-speaking part of Belgium, the Wallonie region, has put in place two programs to achieve this.

In one, the SME applies for a grant to carry a specific project involving a master degree student. Working either in the firm or in the university laboratory, the student maintains close contact with the firm. The project must combine the educational need of a structured project with the relevance to the firm's ability to succeed in the market. These apparently opposed requirements must be reconciled, requiring a dialogue between university professor and firm's manager in a positive and open-minded spirit, with a common and true interest in contributing to the local business environment. It takes particular faculty members to be sufficiently aware of the SME's business environment and to see the value in providing them with the collaboration of graduate students. The regional government pays 70 per cent of the engineer's salary and of the university support for the project. Projects last, typically, two years, at the end of which the engineer is often hired by the SME.

In another program, the SME obtains 'innovation vouchers' (up to €20,000 per annum) to be used in public research centers towards resolving specific technical problems.

The programs mentioned are non-bureaucratic and can be implemented quickly. They make it possible to carry out successful projects, mainly because the initiative is 'bottom up', emanating from an identified need by the SME. Such projects often lead to positive outcomes for the market position of the company. Also, the graduate students discover that SMEs may offer attractive places to work and close to 60 per cent of them are hired by the firm at the end of the project.

A similar institute for the promotion of innovation and science and technology was established in the Flemish part of Belgium in 1991. It has a budget of €200 million. These programs seem quite effective in catalyzing the rapprochement between SMEs and university research staff.

As illustrated by the above examples, in the last 15 years or so, regional governments have increased their help to SMEs, particularly with innovation projects, because this contributes to maintaining and developing employment in the region. This makes sense because geographical proximity remains an asset, even in our internet age – we often hear the buzzword 'clusters'. This assistance will grow more effective, as regional governments acquire a better sense of the dynamics of business and of world markets.

At the national level

For full-time employment, many UK universities make a special effort to encourage students to apply for jobs and join SMEs. Let us look at the case of the high-performing University of East Anglia, in Norwich, England. In passing, let us note that this large university is very active in research collaborations and in technology commercialization, particularly in the area of life sciences. Also, it attracts many students from Asia, as it has a very good reputation in China and India, in particular. Its website (www.uea.ac.uk) has a section that presents a very positive picture of work in a SME. This section concludes on what an SME offers (more autonomy and responsibility at an earlier stage, space for more creativity, a less bureaucratic environment, etc.). It also underlines that university graduates must explain their role and potential contribution to the management of the SME, which may not be used to hiring graduates.

As another example, the Netherlands' Ministry of Economic Affairs offers 'knowledge vouchers', essentially subsidizing SMEs to buy research from universities. A voucher is worth €7,500 euros; a third of this sum is paid by the SME. This scheme has met with considerable success; so much so that, in 2007, there were 6,000 such vouchers in place. This program is similar to the Belgian initiative described above. In 2009, Switzerland introduced a similar scheme.

At the international level

The European Union has several programs specifically addressed to provide expert professionals to SMEs. One of them is the Marie Curie Programme, by which researchers from public laboratories or universities are seconded to firms, smaller firms in particular. There is a 'mobility' stipend to the researcher of €500–800 per month, plus funds for equipment, in the case of SMEs.

A specific example of a SME–university collaboration involving graduate students

The following example illustrates what an SME can do to benefit from the inputs of students. HiFiPower is a small company in Copenhagen. It is active in audio power conversion and it has a program involving.[6]

This company has 40 employees and invites 20 master's students each year to come and work with the employees over a period of a few months. The work is the object of a thesis for the student, carried out in the last semester of a master's degree. The program is based on the belief that exploratory work towards breakthrough innovations is best done by external, fresh minds. Thus, the technical developments selected are also studied by staff working in various universities.

Well before coming for their traineeships at the firm, at the beginning of the master's course, students are briefed on the technical roadmap and priority areas of interest of the company. Then, one or two managers from the firm teach a few sessions in the master's course. Finally, a selection is made of the students who will be doing their thesis work at the company. Most years, one or two students are hired for permanent jobs.

Since its creation in 2000, HiFiPower has steadily grown. A majority of its revenues today are not in its initial sector of activity. Involving young external players has resulted in a host of new products serving a variety of sectors.

An obstacle to SME–university partnering

As discussed above, special incentives must be put in place in order for SMEs to fully take advantage of inputs from university R&D. These aim at overcoming their relative scarcity in personnel and funds and enhancing what is sometimes referred as 'absorption capacity' of smaller companies.

There is another obstacle to such collaborations. Universities or laboratories selling technical services incur high selling costs to secure contracts, as mentioned earlier. It is not much more expensive to sell a €300,000 project than a €15,000 project. The temptation for the university provider is to prioritize larger companies with deeper pockets, which can afford large projects. To overcome this bias, especially attractive financial incentives of the types described in the previous section are necessary. In fact, universities must be fully aware of such sources of funding, so that they can offer the SME both a project to solve the issue at hand and the way to help finance it.

A prerequisite for all this is that faculty members feel motivated to work with SMEs. This is far from granted, as professors often prefer to work with managers from corporations, who bring them, they feel, more worthy problems. In order to cater specially for the needs of SMEs, Switzerland created a chain of higher schools (HES) a few years ago.

Faculty members within business schools are also often not very interested in developing case studies with local SMEs. A more positive attitude would help them to understand that preparing such cases provides a close interaction with the management of the SME. This results in a mutually beneficial learning exercise, which may provide important insights, on marketing, for example, for the SME and on the management practices and culture for the faculty member. Used in the classroom, such case studies will alert students to the specific world of SMEs and may ignite their interest to work in one of them, rather than the more impersonal, large corporation. Business schools specifically focused on entrepreneurship, such as Babson, USA, EM Lyon, France, Sankt Gallen, Switzerland, as well as several universities in China and Taiwan, have a special interest in small companies and their particular circumstances.

Let us now turn to specific situations prevailing in several countries.

Germany

The Mittelstand companies are often saluted as a key element of Germany's success as the world's second largest exporting economy, after China. They tend to dominate a niche in the market and to be good both at understanding customers and at innovating in a coherent long-term perspective. This is partly due to the fact that a substantial fraction of them are controlled by families, which are oriented towards the long term and are not subject to the whims of the short-term perspective of the stock exchange and financial analysts. Typically, Mittelstand firms have a very low debt burden.

Germany is one of the countries in the world, together with China, which seems serious about developing a strong 'green technologies' sector, as a way to create jobs and to save the planet. Mittelstand companies constitute key actors in this area. In the solar energy sector, for example, Germany has invested close to €200 million in 2008 alone. In the general sector of 'green technologies', it is estimated that Germany has invested €5.5 billion in 2009. As a result of the 'Initiative for Excellence' of the German government, additional funding has been made available to SMEs to partner with universities, particularly in areas aimed at enhancing the sustainability of our economic system.

Finland

Finland is usually considered as a country which, together with Switzerland, handles knowledge and technology transfer well. With regards to SMEs, Enterprise Finland is a web-based service for this type of companies. Managed by the Minister of Industry, it provides a portal for all information useful during the life of a company. The service-specific site presents what SMEs can obtain from nine organizations participating in this service: Finnvera, Finpro, the Foundation for Finnish Inventions, the National Board of Patents and Registration, the Finnish Innovation Fund (Sitra), the Finnish Industry Investment, the Finnish Funding Agency for Technology and Innovation (Tekes), Employment and Economic Development Centers (TE Centers), and the Finnish Tax Administration.

Of these agencies, particularly relevant to the present purpose is Tekes, the main public funding organization for research, development, and innovation in Finland. Every year, Tekes finances close to 3,100 R&D projects, and almost 600 public research projects at universities, research institutes and engineering schools. The agency does not claim any intellectual property rights. Its budget was €516 billion in 2008, which functioned as matching funds: it thus helped finance projects representing a total of €1 billion. An increasing share of Tekes funding is allocated to projects launched by SMEs Of all the funds granted to companies in 2008, a significant majority (80 per cent) went to firms with fewer than 500 employees. Support was introduced in 2008 to accelerate the growth of young companies.

Consistent with our leitmotiv that non-technical innovations are very important to ensure competitiveness of the enterprises, it is worth noting that Tekes has recently shifted a significant amount of its resources towards 'non-technical developments', as stated by its director general: 'In 2008, 37% of funding by Tekes was already directed to non-technical content and 23% to service-related innovations. Work continues with customer relationship management and related reforms of offering descriptions and customer care models, training and tools development.'[7]

Sweden has an agency, Vinnova, similar to Tekes. In its 'research and growth' initiative for SMEs Vinnova provides funding for feasibility studies and specific development projects. More than 100 firms benefit every year from a support which represents a total of €11 million. Here also, the firms provide matching funds for the project.

In addition, VTT Technical Research Centre of Finland is the largest contract research organization in northern Europe. Its turnover is €225 million per year and its staff 2,700. More than a third of the budget is covered by government funding. A fair number of its activities are targeted at Finnish SMEs.

China encourages SMEs to engage with universities

There are 3.25 million enterprises in China. Out of these, 81 per cent have fewer than 50 employees. It is estimated that only 120,000 SMEs (less than 4 per cent of the total) can be termed 'innovative' and thus be candidates for partnering with universities to go from science to business.

In China, SMEs are seen to constitute a crucially important source of new jobs. As a result, national policies aim at encouraging small companies to collaborate with universities on projects which may help them become more competitive. In China, SMEs refer to enterprises where the number of staff is less than 2,000 with annual revenue under RMB300 million.

The Torch Program, started in 1988 by the Ministry of Education and Science and Technology, is primarily aimed at helping SMEs better benefit from university research. For example, it defines the policies (tax holidays, subsidies for training) affecting China's 500 science parks and incubators promoting entrepreneurship and technology transfer towards the companies located in the park or in the region.

As an example, corporate taxes for firms established in these parks are 15 per cent instead of 25 per cent. Also, the Torch Program provides subsidies for training courses offered in these locations. Indeed in China, science parks and incubators see themselves as a platform for training, providing extensive courses and seminars. It is difficult to really assess the quality of these educational programs, but it is remarkable to note the proliferation of courses offered in each location.

Each Chinese province has a Science and Technology Committee, which, among other tasks, helps SMEs secure monies from an Innofund of $0.5 billion, in order to fund firm–university collaborations. Additional funds ($0.2 billion) are also available from the central government.

All in all, there is an arsenal of measures available to support and help SMEs keep abreast of technical development and remain competitive, in order to protect employment. However, an equal, or even higher priority seems to be for Beijing to foster the development of national champions, often controlled by the state. For example, these receive low-interest loans to help finance acquisitions or international development.

In the fall of 2009, the Chinese government announced a new series of measures to foster SMEs. In particular, procurement rules will raise the amount of purchases of commodities, engineering and services from SMEs. In addition, tax breaks to small firms with an annual taxable income below RMB30,000 yuan ($4,390) will be granted for the year 2010.

The Republic of Korea

The Korean government communicates a lot about how small companies are the engine of growth for the country. At the same time, Samsung accounts for about 15 per cent of the country's GDP, a proportion similar to that of Nokia in Finland.

As in many countries, smaller companies in Korea do not have enough of a global mindset. As a result, they do not leverage international markets effectively. The government recently announced a plan to change this and help develop 300 international 'champions' in Korea. In order to help in this, the Ministry of Knowledge Economy has stepped up its efforts to provide advice on this issue, among other via a website (www.gobizkorea.com), which provides information on non-Korean markets. The agency Small and Medium Businesses Corporation (SBC), founded in 1979, is increasing the financing available for international growth. Universities and agencies, such as KITECH, or KAIST, provide partnerships and assistance as necessary.

Taiwan

Taiwan is very heavily dependant on its fabric of strong SMEs. It is also economically very connected with the three largest economies in the world: USA, Japan and China, with which Taiwan is currently negotiating a free trade agreement and where more than 1 million expatriated Taiwanese managers work. With few large corporations, the export-led Taiwanese economy relies heavily on SMEs. Most Taiwanese universities have a faculty of management and entrepreneurship well accustomed to being in contact with and contributing to SMEs.

The overall policy of the Taiwanese government, not surprisingly, aims at moving SMEs from (relatively) low-cost manufacturing to the status of 'innovative R&D'. For this, the Agency for SMEs of the Ministry of Economic Affairs (www.moeasmea.gov.tw) has set up a number of incubators, managed by universities, for managers of SMEs to interact with the faculty, their peers (the agency calls this 'mutual assistance') and have training as well as access to information on how to access to loans and funding.

In addition, this agency has set up an on-line SME university, which seems to have encountered real success. This web-based learning (www.smelearning.org.tw), launched in 2003, has had 2 million visits per year over 2008 and 2009. Courses are offered on a variety of specific topics in the usual areas of management: strategy, finances, marketing, innovation and R&D management, manufacturing, information technology, human resources, as applied to the particular circumstances of SMEs. They also include skill courses, such as Japanese or English language, graphic arts and design, as well as presentation skills.

Many years ago, the government developed excellent infrastructure in 'industrial parks', where ex-pats working in the USA were attracted to settle, join small companies or start their own.

Fostering SMEs in Singapore

The city-state of Singapore is well known as a financial center. It is also a powerful transportation hub (harbour and airport), as well as a large actor in the petrochemical industry. It is also a substantial manufacturing site, in particular for electronics components. As an example, Singapore has a large market share in the world production of hard discs for computers.

Based on this activity, the government of Singapore, through its agency the Economic Development Board (EDB), has been conducting a consistent policy aimed at moving the activities of the state further up the value curve. This includes the support of education, including the National University of Singapore (NUS) and engineering schools. It also includes attracting research laboratories of large multinational corporations. Finally, part of this policy is to favour the creation and growth of start-up companies, as well as attracting SMEs from outside the country and supporting those within the country. A comprehensive program in favor of SMEs is managed by the government agency Spring Singapore, thus enabling this enterprise. This program includes several components, as follows:

- Financing: an arsenal of loans are available, from micro-loans for companies having less than ten employees, to a local enterprise finance scheme, providing loans up to $15 million to allow upgrading and expending the business.

- Capability development: executive education courses are offered to specifically fit the needs of managers of SMEs. Also advisory services, as well as funding are available to technical SMEs to contribute development of offerings or of the operations of the SMEs.
- Access to markets: a number of websites are available for SMEs to learn about the implications of free trade agreements, as well as procurement opportunities offered by a large number of government agencies. Other portals provide opportunities to tap into a large community of customers and suppliers. In addition, a general information website is available at www.business.gov.sg.

In support of these specific measures, the Singaporean government is also practicing a policy of encouraging the entrepreneurial spirit in the population. This starts with high school education where individual initiatives, teamwork, and project-based activities are encouraged. One way to achieve this is to train teachers how to effectively conduct this type of activity and to discuss with them the role and importance of entrepreneurship. The Singaporean government is one the world's most active in undertaking such comprehensive efforts to promote entrepreneurship in the country.

The example of Italy, another SME-intensive economy

Like Taiwan, Italy is a developed economy heavily dependent upon SMEs. In particular, northern Italy is well known for its 'districts', which are regions concentrating a large number of SMEs involved in the same industry: textiles, shoe-making or machinery, for example. Many connections link these firms, even if they are competing, as they tend to behave like a team, flexible and agile to respond to the demands of the market. If a plant has spare capacity, it rapidly helps out another company with a peak of orders. There is also the issue of SMEs partnering with universities or public laboratories, in order to become more competitive and profitable.

In recent years, Italian universities have been severely under-funded. They are therefore inclined to look for additional financing from external sources. The regional governments are encouraging this, as they increasingly promote the reprofiling of their economic environment. This is particularly the case in the regions of Lombardia and Veneto, in northern Italy.

Parallel to the university R&D and often closely connected with it, Italy has some 100 research institutes of the Consiglio Nationale delle Recherche (www.cnr.it). The latter has 9,000 employees in total and does research in a multitude of fields. Depending upon the institute, there is a certain amount of R&D partnering with SMEs, either directly on a one–to-one basis, or via the ongoing seventh European Union Framework Programme.

As an example, one of the CNR institutes, IMEM, in Parma, is developing devices aimed at improving energy efficiency in man-ufacturing processes. This is done in collaboration with SMEs from the area, with a financial contribution from the region of Lombardia. Another example is IMAMOTER, also a CNR insti-tute, with a main location in Ferrara. Its staff is specialized in carrying out applied research for agricultural and earth-moving machines and offering services to these firms. A considerable fraction of the funds of the institute come from contracts with multinational companies, as well as from SMEs active in the region, which includes an industrial district with a large concen-tration of interacting SMEs in this sector. The institute provides services to these firms, including certification of systems and machinery.

There is a fair amount of debate about the competitiveness and the ability of the business model in northern Italy to adapt to novel business practices in the context of intensified competi-tion from China, India and Vietnam, in particular. A recent paper studies the innovativeness and productivity of Italian SMEs.[8] It concludes that Italian SMEs, although they invest less in R&D than their EU counterparts, are nonetheless no less innovative. They are rather more productive per employee, as well.

About ten years ago, Italy instituted an independent agency, with the mission of evaluating 'the efficiency and effectiveness' of universities. This appears to follow the example of the UK approach of evaluation, discussed in Chapter 6. This National University Evaluation Council (www.osservatorio.murst.it) is part of the Ministry for Research and Technology. Indeed, a component of the evaluation is the relevance of universities to large companies, as well as to SMEs.

Chile

With an economy generally considered as one of the most open in the world, Chile is a prime exporter of copper and salmon. Although it has a strong set of SMEs, these represent only 4 per cent of the value of the country's exports, 96 per cent being accounted for by large firms. Tax incentives are available to promote exports by smaller companies. The Ministry of Economy controls the development agency CORFO, which is largely focused on SMEs. The latter have the Banco Estado to provide loans, but Chile's firms complain that they do not have sufficient access to financing.[9]

A number of firms have emerged from universities, especially in the usual ICT and biotech sectors. They have the USA as their principal market, benefiting by being in a similar time zone as most of the country. The agency Fundación Chile, a non-profit private organization for the promotion of innovation in small firms, in particular, put together consortia involving universities (www.fundacionchile.cl). As in many countries, however, there is generally some tension between the universities and the economy and industry.

Not-for-product development alone

Most of the examples above deal with product innovations. A technical context is implied by the phrase 'technology transfer'. It is, however, clear that SMEs must also interact with universities on topics which have nothing to do with technological development, but everything to do with being successful in the marketplace and more profitable. For example, inputs from university staff can well address ways to improve the customer experience. This input may not be obtained in the course of a 'formal' project or collaboration, but may emerge from a conversation. A marketing professor may well bring useful insights to the owner-manager of a hotel, in order to build a stronger brand and to do a marketing campaign, using web-based tools. Also, a university team may well be effective at providing what is called anthropological marketing, meaning a broad understanding of lifestyles and the way customers behave. Such research activity is particularly relevant for the use of mobile telephony, domotics, particularly with the advent of the new protocol ipv6, and for using ICTs in general.

Universities may also provide insights in other areas of social sciences, especially demographics and health economics, but also societal changes, which may offer new business opportunities. Among these inputs, up-to-date knowledge about a new country where the firm may want to become active might be useful. For example, knowledge on the history, economic development and culture of China will be very useful before making a decision to invest there. Indeed, it is useful to speak with peers and managers from other firms, who have had relevant experience. Academics may provide a broader perspective. Some universities, such as that in La Rochelle, a harbour town on the French Atlantic coast, for example, have focused on the history, culture and economies of China and Malaysia. They are beginning to provide this kind of executive development program in these fields.

SMEs may also learn about the ways customers receive and use their offerings by leveraging the 'electronic space'. This can be done tapping specific websites, or sources of innovations and ideas on new business models, for example, and enquiring on websites such as innocentive or ninesigma (www.innocentive. com; www.ninesigma.com). These sites are electronic forums, where solution-seekers post their problems and enter into contact with problem-solvers, who may have the appropriate solution. If this turns out to be the case, the latter obtains a reward from the solution-seeker.

As noted in a recent OECD report,[10] large firms engage far more in non- technological innovation than do smaller ones. This is a handicap for the latter, since, as mentioned earlier, this kind of innovation may be more central to enhanced competitiveness than a superb, innovative technology, which is not valued by the markets. SMEs must proactively tap into the knowledge and technology of university and public laboratories, not only for technical improvements of products and manufacturing processes, but also for inputs and contributions on business processes, managerial practices and societal trends or concepts. The means that the management of smaller firms should be well aware of who, at what university, is able to deliver such inputs; attending meetings, forums and conferences will provide ongoing exchanges with these particular individuals.

A synthesis from Canada

A recent report from the Canadian Natural Sciences and Engineering Research Council (NSERC) provides a synthesis of the policies proposed to promote collaborations between firms, SMEs in particular, and universities.[11] In this report, the strategy for partnerships and innovation is based on four points:

1. Building sustainable relationships and collaborative projects, facilitated by the NSERC.
2. Streamlining access of firms to universities' knowledge and research. NSERC works with partners to bridge the differences between them: NSERC will modify its existing innovation-oriented policies and programs to make them more accessible and relevant to industry, including revising its intellectual property policy to make it more flexible and supporting the commercialization of university technologies.
3. Connecting people and skills. Industry benefits from employing professionals to assist in the innovation process, including advancing new technologies. Canada's graduates have strong technical skills, but must enhance their non-technical skills (e.g., project management, communication, teamwork) to increase their attractiveness to industry and improve their employment prospects. To help meet the needs on both sides, NSERC will work to place additional qualified candidates within Canadian SMEs, as well as supporting the development of 'innovation skills' (non-technical skills) through research

projects involving businesses working with engineering and science students.

4. Focusing on national priorities. Canada needs to target resources and increase the depth of expertise and talent in priority areas of strategic importance for Canada and Canadian industries. NSERC will support large-scale efforts by leading research groups seizing exceptional opportunities to advance solutions to some of Canada's most challenging economic, environmental and social problems. The approach will be agile and flexible, as recently exhibited by the 'Automotive Partnership Canada initiative'.

This report is very focused on technical development, given the mission of NSERC to provide grants in the science and technical fields. Nonetheless, governments of most OECD countries could take the thrust of these recommendations as their own. What is remarkable here is the intention to have a hands-on approach to place graduate students in SMEs and to support the complete chain of the technology commercialization process, from science to business.

Policies in favor of SMEs: room for improvement

Governments are trying to help SMEs at three levels: national, regional, and local. The measures discussed above concern mainly the national and local levels. At the regional level, the clusters seem to have the favor of the policy-makers. In Japan, for example, 19 clusters have been formed, involving 5,000 firms – mostly SMEs – and 200 universities. The effectiveness of these programs is not altogether clear. Governments seem to be throwing money at the problem and 'communicating' a lot about their initiatives. One of the issues, of course, is that almost nobody in most governments has first-hand experience of the business and management of a small firm. Government officials are more familiar with corporations and tend to favor policies supporting their activity, as has been noted earlier in the chapter. The basic needs of SMEs are to have access to talent, capital, effective business intelligence and managerial advice, as well as up-to-date technologies. These needs are not often met by the governmental initiatives. In spite of this failure, the possibilities of worthwhile inputs from universities are innumerable and the corresponding cost often quite affordable. On their side, small companies must be curious and proactive about seeking information and inputs from such partners.

In some ways, managers of SMEs must emulate the passion for relentless drive for improvement and curiosity displayed by the founders of the Aravind Eye Clinic. In 1976, Dr G. Venkataswamy started the first of a series of remarkable hospitals, in Chennai, in India (http://aravind.org). To attack blindness in India, he developed an organization in such a way that his clinic could perform cataract operations at a small fraction (less than $10) of the usual cost of this intervention in India. This surgery makes use of intraocular lenses, which are produced in-house at an extremely low cost. This chain of eye hospitals is now the largest eye-care facility in the world, treating more than 1 million patients per year. In order to achieve this, Dr Venkataswamy seized every possible opportunity to learn – from university personnel, individual or managers – ways to make its process more effective … and efficient.

When, at the age of 81, Dr Venkataswamy was asked when he was planning to retire, he laughed: 'I do not feel as if this is a job I have to do. I get excited that this can be done.' Aravind is the name of an Indian spiritual leader; this chain of medical SMEs were successful in going from science to cash … with a soul, as it provides affordable eye care for the poor.

This is just one example on the role of less industrialized countries as sources of innovative practices. Western companies must become much less ethnocentric and learn the lessons from these countries. Even without going as far as the extreme, relentless drive for effectiveness of Aravind's management, directors of SMEs are generally highly curious and outwardly oriented. They are constantly in a state of scouting for new prospects, offerings or sources of useful technology. However, more than just the top person in the firm should be mobilized to look out for inputs and ideas from campuses, conferences and trade shows, suppliers, and customers. This should be a concern of everyone involved with the firm.

In brief, governments and universities have still much work to do if they are to effectively promote the competitiveness of SMEs and create jobs as a result. A first requirement is the political will to do this. The agenda of governments must include more attention to these firms. This includes simplifying the rules and considerably reducing the bureaucratic hassles involved in running SMEs, as these represent a very high cost in many countries.

On their side, universities need to be much better prepared to meet the specific requirements of SMEs and to be interested in doing so. They must make a serious effort in presenting their capabilities in ways that are 'legible' by this type of company and university staff must demonstrate a mindset more amenable to serving SMEs, thus contributing to a dynamic of job-creation and the economic prosperity of their region. This must be done without the university running the risk of becoming an agency for regional development, over-dependent upon the region's government. As will be underlined in Chapter 7, it is critically important that universities retain their freedom in deciding how to adapt to their environment by providing excellent learning opportunities, as well as excellent research.

SMEs must be helped in the areas of managerial practices and business intelligence, monitoring markets and technologies, particularly those connected with, energy saving, non-carbon energy sources, and sustainable technologies. As a dynamic part of the economy, they have an important role in accelerating the transformation of our world towards a much higher level of sustainability. Universities, possibly with some government help, may play a stimulating and important role in this area. One way to achieve this is to organize workshops and host forums on specific themes, where managers of smaller firms can learn, exchange, and compare their knowledge or practices.

In this context, the shift noted earlier in the Tekes agency, in Finland, towards increased funding of non-technical collaborative projects, should be monitored. Indeed, the issue, for large and small companies alike, is increasingly shifting to the use technology effectively through appropriate innovative business models, rather than developing new technologies. In all cases, public investments in partnerships must be undertaken with one main goal in mind: job-creation. They must be relentlessly assessed for their effectiveness on that account over the long term.

CHAPTER 6

Best practices for firm–university partnerships

In the previous chapters, we have seen the various ways by which firms enter into collaborations with universities, in an attempt to boost their competitiveness. Let us now look, in this chapter, at what additional helpful steps are required in order to put this complex process effectively into practice within firms; we then look at some framework conditions and or policy issues, which have not been discussed yet.

Then, turning to the macro level, we will compare Europe with the USA. Their performances are similar in the area of knowledge and technology transfer. China, India and Japan are forging ahead, often following their own paths. Finally, the case of Switzerland is discussed, as this country is often shown as an example for its performance in knowledge and technology transfer.

General prerequisites for firms

In order for firms to engage effectively with universities, a pre-requisite is for the firm to be clear about its business developments needs. The next stage is to be aware of what developments need to be carried out in-house and what should be undertaken with external partners. As indicated earlier, the tendency is for increased collaborations. Examples of criteria for this choice are:

- How critical is to have full control of the development?
- The time horizon.
- Is the project more a capacity-building exercise?
- How specific is the development? A scenario involving planning based on geopolitical or societal trends may usually be

conveniently outsourced. Some issues are industry-wide, such as, for example toxicological studies of fine particles emitted by diesel engines. These must be done jointly by the manufacturers of diesel engines.

- What are the returns (cost and risk-sharing, but also climbing a learning curve faster) of going outside?

These criteria are specific to the firm at a given time and must be revisited occasionally. Once this map is drawn up, then the question is: what projects are most suitable for partnering with universities? Finally, what university is most fitted for a given project? Is this university available, contractually and in terms of workload? How customer-friendly is the university, its policies and its KTT office?

A second prerequisite for the firm is the attitude of its staff. An open mind and high curiosity are a must, but they do not come that naturally. There is the general tendency in organizations to be inward-oriented and to consider that the internal resources of the firm are preferable, because they are rooted in the 'culture' of the firm. This is what is described as the 'not invented here' (NIH) syndrome. This can also be accompanied by the fear of discovering that outside resources may be better than anticipated. Technical experts, in particular, tend to have an 'expert syndrome', which make them believe in their superior competence. A well-designed and implemented management development course may act as a powerful agent of change to modify these perceptions and make the staff much more outward-oriented, proactive and curious regarding what goes on outside the firm.

A cosmopolitan staff, composed of individuals from different cultures, literally brings different 'points of view', which are very positive for healthy debates and coming up with new ideas. Furthermore, such staff have connections with persons and institutions everywhere in the world. Thus, they promote a positive circulation of ideas and an openness to outside ones.

One company appears to be very open to external ideas. It is the US healthcare and cosmetic products company Johnson & Johnson (J&J). It has a decentralized structure and an entrepreneurial perspective, where employees are on the lookout for external ideas that can lead to new J&J products. As a result, it is adept at 'internalizing' such ideas and turning them into company successes. Indeed, many of J&J's breadwinning products, such as the supple contact lens, for example, have been brought to the company by external actors, universities, individuals or small companies. If this prerequisite of open mindedness is fulfilled, then the firm will be likely to entertain informal, but sustained contacts with the personnel from the universities most relevant to their business development needs.

In a large firm, an array of 'watchers' regularly exchange information, making sure it is circulated and discussed, in order to best connect with the business. In contrast, in SMEs, only one or two persons watch the university scene, taking into account the 'needs' of the firm. In both cases, experiences are exchanged on the challenges of partnering and managing external collaborations. This is done internally, but also across firm boundaries, as much can be shared on the managerial issues without divulging what specific areas are of interest to the firm's future business.

Issues and expected trends concerning universities and public research organizations will be covered in Chapter 7. With regard to the best practices for the framework conditions, several policy issues are discussed below.

IP Policy

Countries should assign the ownership of patents to the university rather than to the inventor in its staff. In this sense Germany got it right, structuring its law in this direction, whereas Italy went the wrong way by shifting the ownership to the inventor. The rationale is that, in general, universities are better equipped to extract the best value from the patent than are individuals.

However, in the area of patents, it is important to provide resources for preparing and filing them. Also, it is desirable to have a coordination of the patent activity within the firm. This is why the Italian public research organization CNR, mentioned in Chapter 5, should not have decentralized the handling of patents to its individual institutes, especially in the light of the fact that no accompanying budget was provided for them to discharge this new task.

Evaluation of universities

One fair question to ask is whether and how to evaluate universities, in particular with regards their effectiveness at transferring knowledge and technology. The UK is the country that has put in place the most systematic process in this area. Initially this was implemented by the Research Assessment Exercise (RAE), which drove the dynamic by offering increased ranking for the university if it became involved in these collaborations. This exercise did not give recognition to the knowledge and technology transfer activities. It was also resource-intensive in expert time and in management attention, even leading to bureaucracies within the universities to manage the RAE process. The latter has now been replaced by the Research Excellence Framework (REF). This is partly to make the process less costly by using metrics, rather than peer reviews. It also shifts the focus on the impact of the university's activity. The Higher Education Funding Council for England (HEFCE) (www.hefce.ac.uk) stresses the *impact* and 'effective dissemination and application' as key criteria.

The question is how undisputable the metrics used in the evaluation process will be. The REF exercise is likely to encounter some controversy, when looking at the different viewpoints of academia as to how evaluate research performance. How useful is such a tool in achieving real improvement in performance, rather than inducing undesirable dynamics? It is now planned for the REF exercise to start in 2012. Maybe, like other processes, the real value for the universities may be in going through the exercise, as a learning process, rather than in its outcome.

Seed funding

Seed funding consists of providing capital to a new venture, so as to allow it to be in a position of either further funding itself or to call on external investors. This capital is usually used to pay for preliminary operations markets research or early product development. The sources of seed funding are the founders of the business, or family and friends. They may also occasionally be 'angel' investors. Seed capital is not a large amount of money, as many people start up new ventures with sums in the order of €10,000.

Seed funding is different from venture capital investments, which involve higher sums, a much more complex transaction, and a corporate structure that receives the investment. Venture capital therefore comes into play when some of the uncertainties of the venture have been removed, where a reasonable business case can be made for the venture having high growth and profitability in the future. The VC industry has been badly hurt by the 2008 crisis, and this impact may last for several years. In addition, in recent times, voices have been heard to say that the VC industry has become too risk-averse, thus not fulfilling its role.

Seed funding is thus a crucial link in enabling the venture to move forward, as it validates the commercial viability of the offering. It is generally considered that Europe does not have enough sources of such funding available. In contrast, the USA has a number of such sources, such as SBIR, mentioned in Chapter 5, but also a number of non-profit institutions and foundations – the Coulter Foundation, for example. The website www.foundationcenter.org lists the 50 largest foundations, which distributed close to $370 million of seed-money grants in the USA in 2007.

Public procurement

In order to create more 'market pull' for products and services from start-ups and SMEs, a policy encouraging the public sector to purchase these is helpful. In the European Union, roughly 16 per cent of GDP is public procurement. Such a policy provides a positive momentum. Countries such as China, the Netherlands, Singapore, and the USA have taken steps in support of public procurement to this end. Malaysia is considering such a move.

In Europe, the recent EU directive on the Small Business Act, mentioned in Chapter 4, suggests similar measures. It remains to be seen how each European country will translate this into their national legislation. Such a stimulus is helpful, since large companies tend to be conservative in buying goods and services from small companies. As the advertising slogan used to proclaim: nobody has been fired for purchasing an IBM product.

Comparing Europe and North America for their performance in knowledge and technology transfer

Europe and North America are the two most developed regions in knowledge and technology transfer. How do they compare and what are the differences between them?

A ten-year lag

North America developed its network of KTT offices between 1980 and 2000. This increased activity was triggered, in part, by the Bayh-Dole Act, as mentioned earlier. This gave universities more control and responsibility over the management of the intellectual property they generated. It also limited the universities to granting licenses to firms that would predominantly produce the licensed product in the USA.

In Europe, due to the various approaches taken by each country, a more generalized development of technology-transfer (TT) offices took place later, between 1990 and 2000. This difference of ten years has been the main reason for the gap noted by the KTT indicators in recent times. This gap concerned the three vehicles discussed in the previous chapters: collaborative research, licensing, and university spin-outs. Recently, this gap has been steadily closing. Both regions now enjoy similar performances in terms of KTT activities.

In North America, statistics about KTT have been collected by the American Association of University Technology Managers (AUTM. net) for about 25 years. AUTM obtains statistical data for about 200 universities which represent the top 10–20 per cent of the approximately 2,500 universities active in the USA. Of the top 100 universities, 96 are respondents to the annual AUTM licensing survey.

In Europe, the Association of European Science and Technology Transfer Professionals (ASTP) (www.ASTP.net) has been collecting statistical information from its members since 2003. The collected data represents 10–20 per cent of European universities, but not all of the leading institutions are among the respondents. ASTP results would be higher if these universities were included. This will be the case in future surveys.

Similar performances in Europe and the USA

Despite these differences, it is possible to compare the KTT intensity between Europe and North America. Such numbers are expressed per research dollar, in order to take into account the differences in absolute research funding between both regions. The results (see below in the section on Switzerland's technology transfer) show similar general performances.

North American universities are more active in filing patents, partly as a result of higher propensity to patent, cheaper filing fees and a higher number of inventions disclosures received. On the other hand, European universities conclude more licensing deals and generate more start-ups than their American counterparts: as of 2009, 630 in Europe, as compared to 585 in the USA. As already mentioned, the number of start-ups is only one statistic. The really important figure is how many jobs these new ventures are able to create. Reliable data in this area are scarce.

Overall, again, despite the fact that the statistics considered include few of the top performing universities, Europe has a strong performance in KTT-related metrics. This is less so when one tries to assess the performance of firms in commercializing the inventions licensed. As mentioned in Chapter 4, European start-ups do not grow as fast as in the USA. More generally, the lower entrepreneurial spirit in Europe results in fewer successful innovative products on the market. This is likely to explain the lower amount of royalties collected by European universities from the commercialization of their inventions and the smaller number of European companies featured in innovation rankings.

One must, however, remain cautious about these conclusions, since there is no clear-cut indicator able to measure the companies' capacity to commercialize new innovative products. One approach that should be noted is provided by the 2007 European Innovation Scoreboard, which features indicators related to innovation applications and intellectual property creation. The correlation between these two metrics results in the country rankings shown in Figure 3.

Switzerland seems to enjoy strong intellectual property generation. This may be explained by the strong patent culture in the country. It is also due to the fact that this small country is

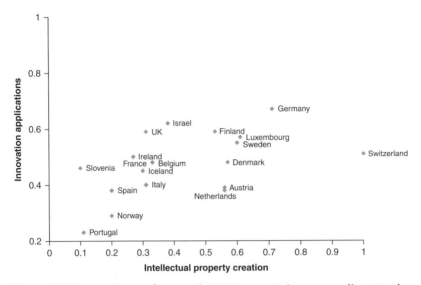

Figure 3 Comparison of several OECD countries, according to the European Innovation Scoreboard (2007)

home to the headquarters of a number of very large multinational companies, some of which are very dependant upon patents, such as Novartis and Roche. Others, such as ABB and Nestlé, also file a substantial amount of patent applications.

However, according to Figure 3, the capacity of Swiss firms to transform such intellectual property in innovative applications is lagging behind other European countries, such as Germany, Finland or Sweden. It is unfortunate that the USA is not included in the evaluation, but the 2007 European Innovation Scoreboard features a specific chapter comparing US and Europe perform-ance in innovation related matters.[1]

Collaborative research

In terms of research partnering between firms and universities, both the American National Science Foundation and AUTM report growing R&D investment by firms in university partner-ships. In 2008, according to AUTM, there were $3.73 billion of industrial research going to universities. This represents roughly 7 per cent of the total research funding of universities, down from 10 per cent in 1999. The National Science Foundation reports $2.87 billion and 5.5 per cent in 2008. A direct comparison with ASTP survey data indicates that industry funds 10 per cent of university research activities.

On a more general level, differences between US and European technology transfer relates mainly to less flexibility in negotiations in the USA. As already mentioned in Chapter 3, Europe may either assign the IP rights or license the intellectual property. This greater range of options may explain the higher intensity of license deals made by European universities, as compared with the USA.

As a conclusion, despite a late start, Europe is now at the same level as North America in terms of KTT output indicators. The differences observed can be explained through cheaper patent costs and differing flexibility in the freedom to negotiation license deals. European firms seem to have more difficulty translating licensing and other technology transfer deals into successful products in the marketplace. We now turn to one of Europe's 'best in class', Switzerland.

Assessing technology transfer: the case of Switzerland

International rankings

Switzerland is enjoying particular (but not widely recognized) success in the worldwide innovation rankings, in first place in the latest European Scoreboard Summary Innovation Index.[2] In terms of competitiveness, it ranks first in the Global Competitiveness Index[3] as well as fourth in the World Competitiveness Scoreboard.[4]

In terms of knowledge transfer and research collaboration between firms and universities, the position is also excellent with a first and second rank for the IMD and WEF respectively in 2010 (see Figure 5).

The progression of the Swiss position in these two rankings is impressive. In about ten years' span, Switzerland progressed from a rank in the 10–15 range to the top spots (Figure 6). What were the main factors responsible for such a progression? In terms of practice, we see a general formalization/professionalization of knowledge and technology transfer that has occurred for the last ten years in Switzerland, mainly through the establishment of dedicated teams working for or within public research institutions (PROs). This is exemplified by the number of technology transfer professionals in Switzerland, as shown in Figure 7 (in full-time equivalent, FTE). Of course, such an increase may simply be the consequence and not the source of the intensification of knowledge and technology transfer, but clearly it has played a role in providing a clear path for companies to establish

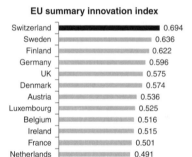

Source: European Innovation Scoreboard, 2009.

Source: Global Competitiveness Report, 2009–2010.

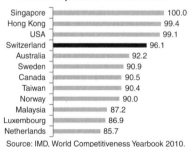

Source: IMD, World Competitiveness Yearbook 2010.

Figure 4 Swiss rankings related to innovation and competitiveness

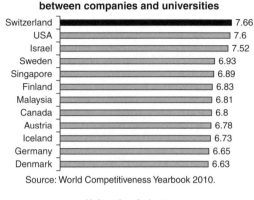

**Knowledge transfer
between companies and universities**

Switzerland	7.66
USA	7.6
Israel	7.52
Sweden	6.93
Singapore	6.89
Finland	6.83
Malaysia	6.81
Canada	6.8
Austria	6.78
Iceland	6.73
Germany	6.65
Denmark	6.63

Source: World Competitiveness Yearbook 2010.

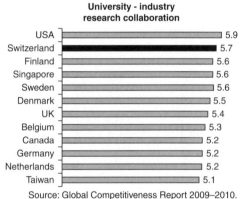

**University - industry
research collaboration**

USA	5.9
Switzerland	5.7
Finland	5.6
Singapore	5.6
Sweden	5.6
Denmark	5.5
UK	5.4
Belgium	5.3
Canada	5.2
Germany	5.2
Netherlands	5.2
Taiwan	5.1

Source: Global Competitiveness Report 2009–2010.

Figure 5 Swiss rankings related to university–industry partnering

partnerships with PROs and for researchers to get clarity on their institution's guidelines when establishing such partnerships.

Deal flow and related metrics in knowledge and technology transfer

Another interesting question when assessing these international rankings is to compare this subjective assessment (based on interviews with stakeholders) with a more objective series of

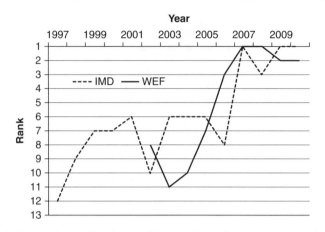

Figure 6 Evolution of Swiss rankings related to university–industry partnering as a function of time

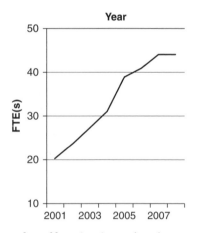

Figure 7 Evolution of staff active in technology transfer
Source: swiTT surveys. FTE = Full-Time Equivalent.

indicators that are based on the intensity of knowledge and technology transfer as compiled by practitioners' professional associations such as swiTT.ch, ASTP.net or AUTM.net through their annual surveys.

These surveys usually cover the following distinctive KTT channels:

- *Technology licensing*, which consists of the transfer through licensing/assignment of research results from the PROs to the firms. The firms (either established or just starting up) buy new technologies from universities in exchange for royalties or other financial considerations.
- *Research partnering* activities, which are established through collaborations between a firm and a PRO around a common research project. Through direct interaction, firms can get access to know how from the PROs and obtain exploitation rights to technologies that may be generated during the execution of the project.

Figure 8 shows the distribution of technology licensing and research partnering channels for Switzerland.

Technology licensing activities are mostly achieved with SMEs as opposed to research partnering activities, which tend to focus rather on large firms and other public institutions. Institutions with more basic, early-stage research (such as universities) tend

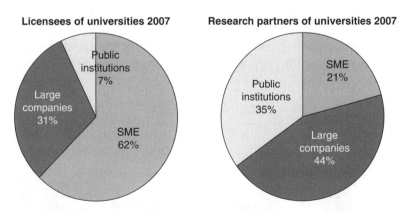

Figure 8 Technology licensing and research partnering channels in Switzerland, by partner type

Source: swiTT survey 2007, which is the most recent survey providing such a comparison.

to prefer to use the channel of technology licensing as compared to institutions with applied research that deploy mostly research partnering activities (such as universities of applied sciences).

We will now address the specific metrics found in each of these two channels of transfer.

Technology licensing

Metrics linked to technology licensing are, typically: the number of inventions made by researchers and communicated to their knowledge technology transfer office; the number of patent applications filed; the number of license deals made with companies; and the number of start-ups created which are based on such license deals (spin-offs).

International benchmarking of technology licensing

In terms of international benchmarking of technology licensing, Switzerland demonstrates a very positive performance, as shown in Figure 9, where comparison is made between the USA (AUTM survey, 2008), Europe (ASTP survey, 2007) and Switzerland (swiTT survey, 2008). Though each survey represents only a subset of the total number of PROs in each region/country, we refer to the corresponding country/region instead of the specific survey in the text below for purposes of clarity. A more in-depth analysis

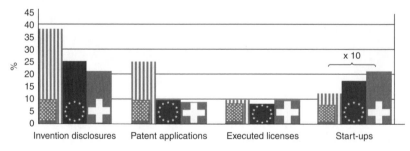

Figure 9 International benchmarking of technology licensing metrics between the USA, Europe and Switzerland

Note: Figures are per R&D budget ($ million): 30% = 0.3 unit for each $ million invested in R&D.

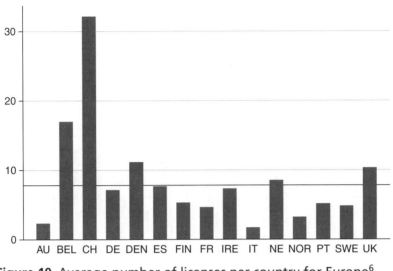

Figure 10 Average number of licenses per country for Europe[6]
Note: n = 185.

on the representativity of these subsets and their comparability can be found elsewhere.[5]

Despite a lower rate of new inventions disclosed by Swiss researchers, their KTT offices are able to convert them at higher rate in executed licenses with firms and through start-up creation. Concurring results have been obtained when benchmarking Swiss technology transfer with other European countries, as shown in Figure 10.

These results indicate that technology licensing is carried out more efficiently in Switzerland than in the USA and Europe. There is, however, room to increase the number of disclosures announced by researchers. Taking into account the high impact of the Swiss research,[7] together with the very high intensity of basic research,[8] one could reasonably expect a large pool of high-quality undisclosed inventions in Swiss PROs. At present capacity, however, it would be very difficult for the Swiss TT offices to deal with such an increase. As shown by Conti and Gaulé,[9] at present, Swiss TT offices would be seriously understaffed to deal with the increased flow of disclosures (assuming a direct relation between publications and disclosures) – see Figure 11.

If hiring more technology-transfer professionals seems to be a solution to overcome this crunch in KTT, the question of the

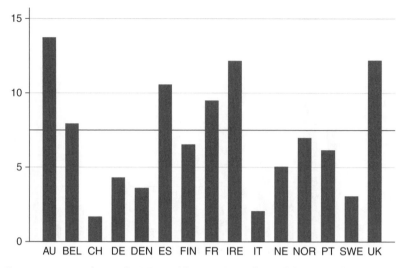

Figure 11 Number of KTT staff per scientific publication by country in Europe

Source: A. Conti and P. Gaulé, *The CEMI Survey of University Technology Transfer Offices in Europe*, working papers series, 2008.

Note: n = 202.

associated costs becomes an issue. Up to now Swiss PROs have supported the vast majority of the costs needed to set up and operate TT offices (roughly CHF 50 million over the last ten years). Most of them could not draw any more resources from their research budget to further develop KTT activities and do not operate at profit in terms of KTT activities.

It should be noted that we did not include in this analysis metrics linked to revenues received by Swiss PROs through the commercialization of their technologies by firms. The reason for this lies in the fact that it depends to a large extent on the ability of firms to commercialize such technologies successfully and hence does not provide a direct measure of PROs' ability to transfer their discoveries. One can, however, note that revenues are much lower in Switzerland (about CHF10 million, according to the swiTT survey, 2007) and in Europe as compared to the USA (where it is more than $3.5 billion, AUTM survey, 2008).

The high conversion rate of invention disclosures into licenses (43 per cent for the University of Geneva since inception as compared to Stanford University's 41 per cent) seems to indicate either a failure of firms to commercialize such inventions or simply that more time is required to generate high revenues from them.

Impact of technology licensing activities for Swtzerland

Despite fewer royalties being collected in Switzerland from technology licensing activities (CHF 10 million according to the swiTT survey, 2007), using a method developed by Stanford University[10] one can evaluate the impact in terms of added tax through corresponding economic growth to about CHF 50 million collected at the Swiss level (2007). The 5x multiplying factor (assuming 50 per cent of the license deals are made with Swiss companies) demonstrates that most of the added value generated by technology licensing lies outside the PROs.

So why, despite even explicit OECD recommendation, has no substantial direct support been provided so far by the Swiss government to technology licensing from PROs?[11] One of the main reasons lies probably in its historical development and positioning. Technology licensing activities have been funded and under direct supervision from PROs. This situation has not provided enough incentive for the government to step in due to the lack of control and leadership for its role. Another reason lies in the limited expertise at hand within the government and its pool of technology-transfer experts who are much more oriented towards research partnering than technology licensing activities. Finally, it should be noted that a similar situation occurred in the past in United Kingdom, where the government eventually stepped in to provide additional support to the PROs under the so-called 'third-stream' funding scheme which has now been active for the last ten years with good success.[12]

Research partnering

The performance of research partnering of PROs with companies in Switzerland is more difficult to assess with precision. The Federal Statistical Office, together with economiesuisse, an

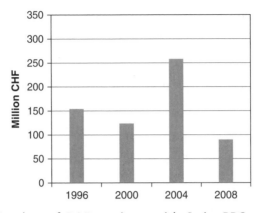

Figure 12 Number of R&D projects with Swiss PROs reported by Swiss firms

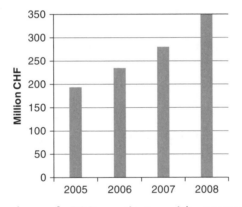

Figure 13 Number of R&D projects with economic partners reported by Swiss universities

association of Swiss firms, conduct, every four years, a survey on Swiss firms' R&D activities. The number of 'extra-muros' R&D mandates to Swiss PROs is reported in Figure 12. It is difficult to define a trend in these results and no monotonic increase in the last ten years has been reported. The situation is different in the case of the data compiled by the swiTT annual surveys (see Figure 13). The reported figures are the amount of R&D mandate cash allocation received by Swiss universities (including the two Swiss Federal institutes of technology) from economic partners (public and private).

The comparison between both figures is difficult because of the different metrics as well as the various time spans of the surveys. Figure 12 comprises all Swiss PROs, in contrast to Figure 13, which only includes universities and the two Federal institutes of technology. On the other hand, Figure 13 not only reports the amounts collected from Swiss companies, as in Figure 12, but also those from foreign companies and public institutions.

International benchmarking of research partnering

International benchmarking of PROs related to research partnerships is more challenging than for technology licensing activities due to the lack of suitable indicators. As an example, PROs cannot be compared on the intensity of their partnership activities since this will depend on whether their focus is on basic or applied research and also their academic culture. Any meaningful comparison would have to be done within a group of PROs with similar profiles, such as universities of applied science, for example.

On the company side, one available indicator related to research partnering is the number of co-publications of firms

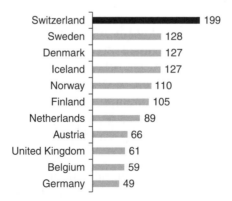

Figure 14 Public–private co-publications per million population
Source: European Innovation Scoreboard, 2009 (based on 2007 data).

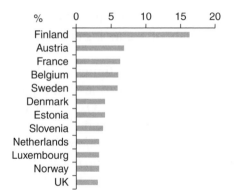

Figure 15 SMEs collaborating on innovation with higher education institutions, as percentage of all firms
Source: OECD STI Scoreboard, 2009.

(located in a chosen country) with PROs, per million of population. As depicted in Figure 14, Swiss firms rank first. The density of the Swiss research with regards to its population clearly provides an advantage here. It would, however, be more meaningful to measure the share of co-publications with firms in comparison to the total number of publications. This indicator is, however, interesting in the sense that it also includes not only technology but also knowledge transfer between firms and PROs.

In the case of SMEs, several indicators measure the intensity of their interaction with PROs. The percentage of SMEs collaborating on innovation with higher education institutions is shown in Figure 15.

Unfortunately Switzerland is missing from this ranking. It is, however, possible to estimate the percentage based on the fact that SMEs represent between 30 per cent and 40 per cent of the total amount of Swiss PROs projects with firms (swiTT surveys, 2005–7). The resulting computation gives us between 3 per cent (10 per cent x 0.3) and 4 per cent (10 per cent x 0.4).

Such an evaluation positions Switzerland in second place in the tier of countries in Figure 15.

This result fits with the generally poor performance of Swiss SMEs in terms of R&D intensity (Figure 16) and innovation co-operation (Figure 17), where Switzerland's performance is below par in comparison with its European counterparts.

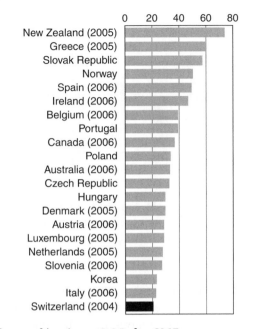

Figure 16 Share of business R&D for SMEs

Source: OECD STI Scoreboard, 2009 (based on 2007 data).

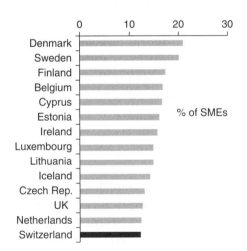

Figure 17 Innovative SMEs collaborating with others, percentage of all SMEs

Source: European Innovation Scoreboard, 2009 (based on 2004 data).

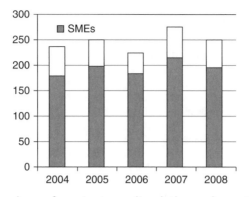

Figure 18 Number of projects realized through matching grants from the government with the corresponding share of SMEs

Source: Annual Reports of the Commission for Technology and Innovation (CTI) Berne, Switzerland.

It is then hardly surprising that, according to an OECD economic survey, SMEs are under-represented in business–university cooperation as well as in cooperation agreements in general: they need to improve what is known as 'absorptive capacity',[13] that is, the capacity to manage and make use of external technical know how.

The lack of involvement of SMEs with PROs, as compared with other countries, is probably partly due to the low level of incentives. Switzerland is one of the few countries that does not allow direct funding of SMEs' R&D by the government. The most widespread tool to incentivize firms (in particular SMEs) to engage with PROs consists of providing matching funds to the firm's own R&D investment in a research partnership project with a PRO. The PRO contribution to the project (usually close to 50 per cent) is funded by the government. Figure 18 lists the number of such matching projects for Swiss firms engaging with a Swiss PRO.

In 2005, the government put in place an initiative to increase collaboration between Swiss companies and PROs through the establishment of KTT consortia[14] aimed at providing companies with easier access to PROs competencies (the consortia became fully operative in 2006 with CHF 12 million provided for the period 2005–7). An impact in terms of increased CTI projects is not visible in Figure 18, where the number of projects remains stable at around 250 per year. This may be due to exhaustion of the (roughly stable) budget made available for such measures each year. However, the number of submitted projects does not increase either (2005: 522, 2006: 407, 2007: 493, 2008: 444), which may suggest that such an initiative, rather than generating new collaborations, streamlines the process of initiation and match-making. As a consequence, other incentives may be needed to increase SMEs' participation in collaborative projects with PROs.

Another level of incentives consists of providing innovation vouchers that allow a firm to acquire R&D credits in a PRO (without the matching requisite). Switzerland has recently started to experiment with this approach. In countries such as Canada,[15] the Netherlands[16] or Ireland,[17] the government provides R&D vouchers to SMEs to allow them to buy R&D from PROs. A review of the effect of voucher has been conducted by Cornet et al. in the Netherlands, which showed a positive effect on firms' absorptive capacity.[18] Other incentives include offering tax cuts linked to R&D investments or providing firms with direct financial support to engage in research partnerships with PROs.[19]

Conclusion: how can knowledge and technology transfer be optimally supported?

Switzerland has achieved impressive results in technology licensing activities in the last ten years. The development and professionalization of TT offices supported by PROs, combined with the excellence of their research, has propelled Switzerland to the forefront of technology transfer world-wide. Technology licensing and research partnering form the two main channels of interaction between firms and public research institutions.

Technology licensing provides good and measurable outputs in terms of deals and spin-offs generated per research budget. Technology-transfer offices are efficient in international comparison but have reached their maximum capacity with the present level of funding. Despite being almost exclusively supported by PROs, technology licensing benefits mainly the government through the collection of tax on the increased economic activity, with an estimated fivefold rate of return.

Research partnering's performance is less evident. Despite positive general indicators, a deeper look points to a low intensity of participation of SMEs. Existing incentives put in place through match-making grants seem to have reached their limit, despite additional actions taken to facilitate the search for partners within PROs through setting up regional KTT consortia.

Increased participation of SMEs in technology-transfer activities with PROs remains a priority. Technology licensing, with its large proportion of smaller firms, provides a good vehicle by which to strive towards this goal. It should also be further developed to fully exploit the potential provided by the Swiss research intensity and quality.

In parallel, new incentives through R&D vouchers and direct R&D funding could generate a more intense participation of SMEs in partnering processes. The United Kingdom, with its ten years of experience of government support for technology transfer, could serve as a source of inspiration for future Swiss funding schemes in this area.

CHAPTER 7

The way forward

Companies and universities belong to two different worlds. Establishing fruitful partnerships between them is often not easy, but this difference must be turned into positive energy. These two actors of the innovation process must increasingly partner effectively to shape the future and respond to change. They join efforts using the three main vehicles discussed in the previous chapters, operating in a very interdependent world. In so doing, they will develop opportunities for wealth and job creation.

Efforts to resolve the many challenges facing the world (energy, water, food, climate change, demographics and healthcare, runaway financial services) provide huge scope for firm–academia partnering in moving the world towards a more sustainable state, while creating new job-generating businesses and services. Much has been achieved, as discussed in the previous chapters, but considerable progress remains to be made. The way forward is outlined below. We begin with a look at corporations.

Large firms

Companies must continue to increasingly look at external inputs to feed and enrich their perspectives and their innovation pipeline. As indicated earlier, firms must federate the capabilities of external actors, thus engaging more in what is called 'open and distributed' innovation. Companies will increasingly be *architects* of innovation for business development. As a result, firms must do a better job of scanning the landscape, as well as undertaking proactive scouting for external contributions, to be integrated into multi-actor innovation projects.

It is possible that, in the future, large firms will make more effort to grow 'organically', as compared to the previous period, where mergers and acquisitions were favored. This is in spite of the fact that such mergers typically do not deliver the promise initially placed in them at the time of their announcement. However, they do make the investment banks richer and, also, often the executives of the companies concerned.

In technology companies, R&D units must be more outward-oriented and proactively scout for external complementary areas of technology. Management must be trusted so that technical professionals will not be penalized for finding external solutions which make them obsolete. Elements of these partnerships are discussed below.

Non-technical inputs

Many of these inputs may not be technical, as products constitute only one element, however important, in the complete business model. Commercial success increasingly demands comprehensive commercial concepts, understanding of societal changes, the potential of the internet, novel distribution channels, as well as innovative offerings. Apple's novel device iPod relies on the innovation of a whole infrastructure (iTunes, etc.) to provide music to roving listeners. ICTs offer broad scope for innovations and novel offerings or services.

More capital-intensive is the electric car, which requires considerable development in battery, control systems and infrastructure to displace the well-entrenched petro-automobile. This holds true even more for vehicles powered by hydrogen fuel cells, which require extensive security installations.

Academics have many useful insights *on ways to achieve a less wasteful society, from urban planning to acceptance of innovations and future societal changes. Firms should be more open and positive about engaging with them. Focus is also required, but primarily it is a matter of mindset, as discussed below.*

Mindset

In this day and age, to be innovative, firms must be able to effectively *federate* many inputs from outside the firm, and combine them with their own internal strengths. The aim is to have a more effective innovation process, energized by entrepreneurial spirit. Large firms, however, are excessively focused on their own activities. They are also very much oriented towards the short term. Finally, financial considerations are driving many mergers and acquisitions that do not fulfill their promise of 'synergy' but instead detract true value-creation from innovation.

Companies must demonstrate much more courage and *curiosity* towards the world outside their boundaries. As is the case with Alice in *Alice in Wonderland* , they must be 'curioser and curioser'.

To catalyze this change, management development constitutes a very effective tool, but the role model and leadership of the management cannot be replaced. The behavior of the staff and the attendant reward systems must be transformed effectively to encourage the taking of risks involved in proactively seeking external inputs. Furthermore, top management must be seen to be taking their full share of these risks. The mindset must indeed be global, with a particular attention to Asia, China and India, as mentioned several times previously.

Courage is needed to engage with universities and public laboratories, among other actors, in order to explore and complement the firms' views of the world. The mindset must also be comprehensive in visioning a more sustainable world. It is not only petrol-guzzling SUVs that are obsolete, it is every aspect of mindless consumption. But, becoming more sustainable is a factor of growth, as well as a force for positive change. There are considerable business opportunities in non-carbon energy sources, for example. We discuss this below.

Scouting

As discussed in Chapter 6, the first thing for the firm to do is to define and articulate its development needs to serve its business development plans. With the general attitude of looking for external contributions, in preparing for effective firm–university partnerships, the scouting activity can then begin. The first step is to identify the universities, faculties or departments which may best contribute to the firms' activities in support of the objectives of the business development plans. To draw this 'map' of potentially useful university and public laboratory sources, many contacts, internally and externally, must be approached for advice. The firm's staff must be consulted on this and, indeed, its board members should also provide suggestions. Managers in other firms may provide useful suggestions as well. The resulting output must then be validated.

This mapping exercise involves a large amount of work when it is done for the first time. Once the map has been developed, the sources identified must be monitored, in order to verify that they are still relevant to the firm. New sources will then be added, as a result of the changing requirements of the firm's business development, as well as the evolution in the external world. As repeatedly mentioned, it is increasingly important to consider universities and public research laboratories as sources of non-technical inputs. Such elements may eventually have as big an impact on the bottom line as a good, new technology.

Scouting for universities as external sources of inputs must be world-wide, as is the case for the other types of external actors, such as suppliers and customers, technology brokers, etc. Large firms locate their innovation/R&D centers in countries presenting large, dynamic markets and talent. Lower cost may be an added advantage, but is not a major reason. With this policy in mind, in the 1950s and 1960s many US firms set up R&D units in Europe. Both the USA and Europe benefited from this.

Nowadays, China and India are countries of choice for locating new laboratories or innovation centers. Following the same logic, western companies will increasingly scout for universities in these countries, in order to benefit from their expertise, insight and innovation by engaging with them at the opportune time. As China and India develop fast and rapidly become major actors in the world's geography of innovation, firms must monitor developments in these countries with particular attention, in order to be able to participate in them at the appropriate time.

If these countries are not familiar to the firm, numerous external sources of information exist: colleagues and managers in other firms, embassies in the country of interest, websites. Certain scientific attachés of embassies may provide very relevant intelligence on the universities, as well as on their ways of collaborating with them. The following countries have the reputation of maintaining active scientific scouting activity thanks to the scientific attachés in their embassies: the USA, Germany, the UK, France, Sweden and Switzerland.

A way to develop global scouting is to use web-based tools. The latter may provide a wealth of data and information on managerial and business practices, as well as specific innovations and technologies. In this category, one of the best-known sites is innocentive (www.innocentive.com). This firm is a spin-off from the pharmaceutical company Eli Lilly. As a result, it focuses on chemical and pharmaceutical topics. Another tool is ninesigma (www.ninesigma.com), which is more generalist. It partners with Procter & Gamble in the effort of that company to boost the number of ideas coming from outside the firm, in its 'connect and develop' initiative. There are numerous other websites, more or less specialized, and the scene is rapidly evolving. The firm must thus keep abreast of the developments in this field, so as to capture the contributions of new sites.

In these innovation websites, solution-seekers place their challenge on the site. Problem-solvers, often individuals in universities or public laboratories, manifest themselves if they believe that they have an approach to solve the issue. Once the contact is made, the solution-seeker provides more information. Following this, if the problem-solver makes an effective contribution, he/she receives a reward from the solution-seeker.

It will be critical to follow how we learn to better use these tools. Currently, there is some 'hype' about their role. They potentially are very powerful. They are not very time-consuming to access, but tap into a considerable resource of individuals world-wide. The firm has to be careful not to divulge critical business intelligence by stating the type of problems it is trying to solve when it calls for the outside world to help. Firms must make sure that their staff experiment with such tools in order to evaluate what potential they might have in providing a useful contribution. Experimentation may be done without investing much time and provides clues as to the relevance of certain specific websites to the prospective search of the firm.

Informal contacts must be developed with the staff of the 'target' universities. Such *conversations* may be held on the occasion of conferences or trade shows. Occasionally, the firm invites selected academics to interact with its staff through a well-prepared forum. Such events are designed to enable discussion of the potential of specific technology-intensive opportunities. External contributions must be used to generate fruitful discussions among the staff regarding the technical and business aspects of the potentially attractive avenues for firm development. Such 'bottom-up' suggestions must be carefully evaluated and meshed with the 'top-down' plans from management for the future. Additional discussions will allow prioritisation of the avenues identified and rejection of inappropriate ones. In these evaluations, also, the university staff may bring useful insights.

In most cases, it is appropriate for the firm to develop its contacts with a given university at several levels: faculty members, staff of the KTT office, the top management of the university – possibly even the PhD students. The firm can, thus, compare the various experiences, in order to have a fuller picture of the circumstances in that particular university and better grasp the possibilities of positive engagement with it in the specific areas of active interest.

Imagining

More than ever, what we need is imagination for positive change. The work carried out by universities and public laboratories is typically supported by government or granting agencies. Their results are, therefore, often far from a stage at which they can be exploited by firms. The latter must therefore take a leap of faith to anticipate the possible contribution of this work. Indeed, universities must go some of the way by projecting the implications of their work into the future and trying to anticipate the possible paths for commercializing their knowledge and technology. Once the firm is aware of the work being carried out, it must do a better job of probing and discussing whether or not it could be deployed, and, if so, where its potential is the greatest.

Imagining must also have to do with enhanced *sustainability*. There are many opportunities in the non-carbon economy, but firms are not very bold at seizing them. Being truly progressive as a force for positive change in this area, with the contribution of the intellectual engines represented by universities and public laboratories, may go some way to improving the calamitous and unfortunate low esteem in which corporations, especially financial institutions, are currently held in public opinion. In contrast, SMEs generally have a much better image.

Engaging with universities and public laboratories

As shown in Figure 1 (Chapter 1), there are many channels through which firms can engage with universities. Depending on the nature of the topic, the industrial sector, and the degree of confidentiality, companies must explicitly select the path(s) they think most appropriate. As an example, in the area of new, non-carbon energy sources, the engagement could take the form of securing a license on a specific, promising technology – say a new generation of voltaic solar cells. It could also take the form of a broad consulting agreement, in order to help define the developments that the firm may consider for its future activities. As indicated earlier, in Chapter 6, firms could learn a great deal from the universities and public laboratories of China and India, in addition to those in Japan.

Much better knowledge management must, for example, foster exchanges among managers within the firm, allowing them to compare experiences on the issues of managing partnerships with academia. Pitfalls and past experiences are thus discussed to improve the effectiveness in developing and managing future collaborations. This ongoing learning process also aims at developing better project leaders, which represent a critical factor to the success of such endeavors, as discussed below.

Leaders of innovation projects

A major bottleneck in firms is the lack of high-performing project leaders. The latter often have a great impact on the success or failure of new ventures. Good leaders and managers motivate people, connect with various actors, have a sharp business sense, a sensitivity to different cultures, are technology-literate, etc. In addition, they must master the art of managing partnerships with external actors. In many ways, they must have a general management perspective. For that reason, leaders of innovation projects could be called 'mini CEOs'.

A proactive development of promising leaders must be put in place in firms to develop the appropriate personnel. This, in itself, may give the firm a competitive advantage over companies that know the scarcity of good project leaders, but are not doing much about it. Not surprisingly, developing effective innovation project leaders actually starts with the recruitment of broad minded, entrepreneurial individuals. Proactive actions then include extensively rotating these individuals across functions and geography, keeping culturally diverse teams, and management encouraging non-conformist, curious behavior.

Firms should stay away from excessively legalistic or constraining frameworks and maintain flexibility in striking deals with universities and public research organizations. They could, indeed, spend large amounts of time and energy scouting and probing external partnerships. They should avoid stretching themselves too far by aligning their business development objectives with monitoring the key sources which they have selected as truly presenting the most potential for partnerships. This sharp focus is even more crucial for SMEs, discussed below.

SMEs

Small and medium-size enterprises (SMEs) should follow the directions outlined above. In addition, their smaller size should make them particularly careful about the following elements. These firms must:

- be very selective in choosing the 'target' universities, as one type of external actors with which the firm may engage. The university must be relevant and attuned to the business development needs of SMEs, while being very motivated to work with them;
- allocate dedicated resources to tracking the activities of universities. A small group of persons should share this task and

regularly exchange views on their finding experiences and plans in this area;

- push the professional associations of SMEs to be more effective at helping identifying potentially useful partners and the ways to work with them;
- participate more in common projects/forums/consortia, which allow exploration and learning in an environment where risks and costs are shared among several participating companies;
- organize well-prepared forums to explore new avenues for business development. This must be done in a spirit similar to that in large firms, as described above;
- use more innovation vouchers, which seem to be a good way to engage with university graduate students on topics relevant to the SME;
- encourage contacts and work with university students and/or 'young' retirees, in a period involving a few years following their retirement.

With regard to policies, in order to stimulate the growth of young companies, public and private organizations should have incentives to buy goods and services from SMEs. Such measures on procurement work well already in several countries. Three main barriers slow down the growth of smaller companies: insufficient access to financing, lack of managerial expertise and of up-to-date knowledge and technology, and not benefitting enough from global markets. Interventions to help the development of SMEs must concentrate on these three elements as priorities and must focus on being effective rather than throwing money at the problems.

In particular, aspects of the SBIR activities, discussed in Chapter 5, should be evaluated and adapted to each specific country. Among these are help in funding developments, and coaching/mentoring the business-development process or entry into a new market.

In many ways, smaller companies and start-ups represent the best force for positive change. They may not have access to large resources, but they have more passion and entrepreneurial spirit, which are the key ingredients to drive change.

Universities

There are some 4,200 higher education organizations in the European Union, as well as some 650 public research laboratories.[1] These institutions represent a great variety of orientation, governance, financing, as well as relevance for and interest in working with companies. They represent a gold mine of knowledge and expertise, which is insufficiently put to work.

This book concerns the segment of research universities, which represent a minority among universities. They are expected to play a progressively growing role as external partners in developing collaborations with firms. This is the result of pressure from society to include commercialization of technology as their third mission. Public opinion may well grow exasperated if the universities are exceedingly inward-oriented. Furthermore, increasing numbers of university researchers are likely to become more interested in commercializing technology. They will thus energize the movement of universities in this direction. Finally, the income from commercialization of knowledge and technology represents additional revenues, although in relatively modest amounts: universities should not count on this to replace substantial portions of income from other sources.

It is generally considered that the best universities, known for their excellence in research and education, are also those which are the most active and successful in commercializing technologies. The examples used in previous chapters, the University of Tokyo, Tsinghua, Cambridge, Stanford and MIT, support this assertion.

The trend towards more autonomy of universities will make them more likely to engage with firms, using the various channels outlined in Chapter 1 (see Figure 1). They should, however, have a proper governance structure. For example, the governing body of the university should not have too strong a representation from the students, as this would turn the president of the university into a political figure, rather than the leader of a learning institution.

More and more, firms are expected to carry out development projects with external partners. The latter, however, must be 'user-friendly', as will be discussed further in this chapter. In this area, the effective use of ICTs is in its infancy and the potential is large. Much progress needs to be made by universities and public research organizations, if they want to effectively create value by partnering with companies. This includes the following aspects.

Towards a more sustainable world

The area of product development certainly contains a tension between the frantic pace of innovation and sustainability. Although it is generally true that the most recent generation of products is more energy and materials efficient (see the cases of cars or computers, for example), companies must aim at those developments which truly result in enhanced sustainability as well as effective value-creation. This means that companies should act responsibly. This may be an unrealistic thing to ask, in view of the tyranny of financial considerations, but:

(1) Inputs from universities may be crucial in providing complementary skills and a broader perspective in the complex area of the 'cradle to cradle' cycle, for example.
(2) Citizens, ever better informed, partly thanks to the internet, will increasingly choose offerings through the filter of their contribution to sustainability, leading the firms providing more wasteful offerings to financial ruin. Citizens/customers have untapped powers to move things for positive change. By aligning millions of acts with their words about sustainability, responsible customers will make a difference. Responsible behavior on the part of customers is a hugely powerful stimulus for firms to become more sustainable. Again here, university education and research have a crucial role in 'guiding' customers and informing a healthy debate.

Another high-priority issue is health. Our societies have a tremendous need for innovations and new concepts, in order to provide quality healthcare at a reasonable cost. We now turn to the specifics of technology transfer from university and public laboratories to firms.

Encouraging the commercialization of technology

University knowledge constitutes a large, untapped reservoir of ideas and expertise to improve the world. Efforts must be made, in order that the third mission of KTT is more positively perceived by the academic world and considered as a much higher priority than it currently is in the large majority of institutions. This includes the fact that, internally, the university staff must become better partners with the KTT office.

The importance of KTT should be signalled by the existence of a vice rector (or vice president) charged with developing this activity. The faculty members involved should be rewarded if they effectively engage in knowledge and technology transfer. The type of reward must be adapted to each institution.

Partnerships with the private sector provide a window on the 'real world', which enriches the university. The latter, however, must keep its focus on excellence in education and research. In the near future, the activity of KTT will progressively develop, in amount and in priority, but, in many cases, it may remain relatively marginal, as compared with education and research. A wide spectrum of possibilities exists for the universities to position themselves in balancing the three missions.

The KTT office

The professionalism of the staff in KTT offices must increase. Care and concern to attract and retain good staff are first requirements. Furthermore, in many universities, the KTT staff have become insufficient in number, but the funds are lacking to expand the office. This is unfortunate, since, in most universities, many more commercialization deals could be concluded if this bottleneck was removed and additional staff were available to develop the activity. Investments to correct this situation are most likely to come from public sources, with clear objectives assigned to the KTT office, when the funds are granted.

Managing and rewarding the KTT staff in a sensible way must be a priority. The incentives and rewards must be carefully devised, so as not to create perverse effects or undesirable outcomes. Again, here, these must take into account the specific character of each institution. The staff must be flexible and have a deal-making ability to negotiate with the firm and the university researcher.

In terms of structuring the activities of the KTT offices, there is no unique model and, therefore, as often in management, no panacea. The KTT offices are often small: five professionals or so. Generally, among the three main channels for commercialization (collaborative research, licensing and spinning out), KTT offices must maintain a good level of specialization and not spread their activity too thin. For example, in one KTT office, a unit should specialize in licensing and another on collaborative research projects. This is the way the Stanford's office is structured. Each unit has its own competencies but is coordinated with the activities of the other unit. This, of course, is possible in the case of Stanford, which has more than 30 staff, but would be difficult in so many KTT offices with only three to five employees.

KTT professionals must increasingly cultivate a trusting relationship with the university researchers. They must take the time to engage with them and to listen to their advice. If not, a critical element of the effectiveness of the knowledge and technology transfer will be missing. The partnerships between the KTT office and university researchers will become more critical in the future, as researchers become increasingly interested in commercialization of technology; if they do not respect the work of the KTT office, they will be tempted to bypass it.

The profile of the staff in the KTT offices must be constantly reassessed. The role of organizations (AUTM in the USA; ASTP in Europe) must be stepped up in this regard. An example of a course for technology professionals, organized by ASTP, is given at www.astp.net. This three-day course was offered in 2008 in Vienna, Austria.

These professional associations are expected to act more as sources of knowledge, exchange and advice, as well as providing guidance on the most appropriate management-development programs available to these professionals.

An external KTT office?

A trend could be that a company may be contracted by several universities to develop collaborative projects in a given technical area. The company would tap into the expertise and equipment of the universities in that area, secure firm-supported projects and retain an overhead fee to manage the development projects. In this case, the company would play the role of a middle-person, bridging university researchers and firms. Here also, particular care must be taken to make sure that the ownership and rights on the intellectual property situation is clearly defined.

Providing guidance to doctoral students

Boundary-pushing research work, carried out in the course of doctoral theses, is the most amenable material for commercialization. It is therefore important to alert PhD students to the possible applications of their work and to make them sensitive to confidentiality and to the patenting process.

This work of interacting with the population of doctoral students may be undertaken by the staff of the KTT office, or by faculty members from an entrepreneurship center. For example, this is the practice of the entrepreneurship center of the University of Cambridge. In parallel, faculty members themselves must be made more receptive on these issues, through informal discussions and specific workshops.

Making universities more user-friendly

Most universities have a long way to go if they want to become more effective partners for firms. In addition to the crucial requirement of a *mindset* favorable to the activities of commercialization of knowledge and technology, specific steps must be taken:

- The university website must provide clear information to firms as to how to approach and engage with it.
- A clear, one-stop approach must be developed for the various channels for commercializing technology. This must be reflected in the website
- Program directors should be designated, who will act as an interface with firms on broad themes, such as energy or transport. These directors will know the activities pertaining to these

themes in the various departments and will therefore help the firm find orientation in what is a fragmented scene.

- Appropriate training must be provided to the staff involved in operating at the interface with firms.
- A non-bureaucratic, streamlined and flexible process should be developed at every step of the relationship between firm and university. Please see following section for further details.
- In particular, the contractual guidelines and IP policy must be clear and flexible enough to adapt to each particular situation.

Fighting bureaucracy

A recent study in the UK indicates that it is becoming increasingly difficult for industry to collaborate with academia.[2] This study begins by drawing the attention to the fact that firms find it increasingly difficult to work with universities, despite many government initiatives designed to increase such partnerships.

On the other hand, the study indicates that informal relationships between scholars and business people have increasingly come under scrutiny and oversight by university administration. Universities' officials, sometimes TTOs, are increasingly seeking to capture the value of IP. According to businesses responding to the study, these officials often have unrealistic expectations about the economic value of the work they are helping negotiate. Half (49 per cent) of the respondents felt universities overvalued their IP. Over half of the respondents (55 per cent) blamed administration and regulations, including confidentiality, the ownership and value of IP, for limiting their collaboration with universities.

Similar comments have been expressed in the past by managers of US companies concerning partnering with universities. Putting aside the self-serving nature of certain of these comments, it is critical that universities find a balance between their own interests and their role of serving companies and society as a whole. They must not be excessively 'greedy'. Also, the natural dynamics of bureaucracy must be combated with energy. For this, rules and regulations must be constantly monitored for possible, negative, unintended consequences that would get in the way of effective partnerships and true value-creation.

Segmentation of research universities

Among research universities, a dynamic of segmentation is most likely to prevail. One segment includes the more 'basic', early-stage research universities, such as the university of Cambridge (which has the world's highest number of Nobel laureates), Caltech, or the University of Tokyo. These institutions are the source of discoveries which take a fairly long time to be turned into new businesses, but are most likely to have a large impact. The science-based business of pharmaceuticals and biotechnology is an example of this.

Another segment is constituted by universities carrying out applied research and technological adaptation or improvement, vital for the competitiveness of firms.

The third segment is the regional university, which, by its governance and its funding, is strongly encouraged to work with SMEs in the region in which they are located.

This segmentation will not be absolutely clear cut, as each university is likely to retain a mix of characteristics, but the trend to some kind of specialization is expected to intensify, largely as a result of the increased autonomy of universities.

The research universities and public research organizations constitutes a natural focus of attention in the European Union's approach to knowledge generation and innovation. Several concerns have been raised in this context in a recent EU publication.[3] They deal with questions, such as: (a) How can more EU universities be at the forefront of international research to be able to provide EU firms and governments with the best and most relevant research findings? (b) Do EU companies have the capabilities needed to scout and capture the research output of the region's university faculties and trainees?

Universities reaching out

Universities will have to invent new, effective ways to attract firms to enter into interactions with them. Ongoing developments, such as the Hauser Forum at the University of Cambridge, across from the famous Cavendish laboratories, offer examples of this. The building, the construction of which started in October 2008, will provide a space for university and firms to exchange and hold forums. This will have a very useful purpose, and there was a need in Cambridge for such a space for exchanges. The key factor, however, is an effective 'management' of the connections, contacts, interactions, forums and workshops involving firms and universities, in an attempt to generate fruitful and vibrant *conversations*, ultimately, possibly, leading to collaborations. The appropriate persons with adequate resources must be provided, in order to orchestrate and stimulate such conversations by setting up appropriate events. This is more important than buildings and physical plant.

Universities teaming up

A possible trend is to have several universities group themselves to share a common KTT office. The aim is to introduce economies of scale and to have access to a larger pool of expertise and 'deal flow', in the case of potential start-ups. The Innovation alliance between Trinity College and University College Dublin is an example of this. The objective is to improve the outcome of public funds in research. It is hoped that 300 new firms, employing 30,000 persons, will be established within ten years. Government funding of €65 million per year for ten years has been announced. A dedicated technology venture fund is also planned.

Once the universities are collaborating and that their respective research teams know each other, then they can share a common KTT office. Doing the reverse, that is, imposing on several universities the use of the same KTT office, is likely to be counterproductive, since the researchers will not have established a prior rapport with the KTT staff.

An alternative to this kind of alliance is to provide mechanisms and incentives for encouraging the collaboration of researchers belonging to different institutions. This 'organic' process may take some time, but it may be effective in due course.

University spin-outs

In incubating university spin-outs, appropriate external managerial know how and business knowledge should probably be called upon to help pull projects towards commercial success. To succeed on this most complex path for going from science to business, the university must have access to the necessary competency. This primarily concerns enlisting high-performing entrepreneurial teams, guidance, and coaching so that they best navigate the development of their venture, while accessing the relevant business network and to the investors' community.

New ventures should not be prematurely incorporated into companies. In particular, seed money should be available to validate the commercial validity of the projects. It is important to emphasize here again that the critical criterion of success of the spin-out process is, not so much the number of spin-out companies formed, but rather the number of jobs created downstream by a healthy growth of the ventures.

Universities: changes over the long term

In the longer term, universities are likely to have to pursue several paths in order to become more effective partners with firms looking for new activities. These are outlined below.

Development of a more outward orientation

Research universities must become more curious about the outside world, particularly the world of firms. It must develop a better knowledge and understanding of the business world. This will be done by hiring personnel, but also by engaging with firms in different ways, as mentioned previously. Rotation and secondments between companies managers and faculty members are likely to be more frequent and better accepted by both parties.

Leverage business schools to enhance KTT

Research universities often have a business school as one of their faculties. The business school should be encouraged to provide guidance and expertise to the university, in particular when it concerns the commercialization of technology to create new business. This change begins by hiring faculty members who are compatible with these tasks in the first place. Too often, business schools ignore this aspect, concerning themselves only with topics of little relevance to the process of business creation from innovation in general and the linkage between firms and university for value-creation, in particular.

Get rid of the silo mentality

One of paradoxes manifested by universities is that these knowledge-creating institutions are generally poor at managing knowledge-creation and -enrichment, with a view to improving their effectiveness and impact. This is largely due to the fact that academics accept very little interference by any managerial activity in their research activities. Also, academics prefer to concentrate on their own specialized topics, on which they interact with colleagues in other institutions, rather than with their peers within their own university. As a result, they often miss potentially innovative home-grown collaborations.

On the other hand, the nature of such academics is that they have enormous need for autonomy, typical of researchers in any field. The danger of imposing too much management is that it can destroy the creativity, motivation and quality of the staff. A delicate balance must thus be found between total chaos and 'corralling' academics. When this balance is not tactfully found, the management is rejected.

More than ever, tomorrow's problems will not be limited by disciplines and faculties within universities. They are transdisciplinary by nature. Thus, they must be tackled as projects including a diversity of competencies. Such an issue-based perspective, which is typical of firms' organization on multi-disciplinary projects, is resisted by many faculty members because it is perceived as a loss of their autonomy.

Escaping from this silo mentality will require much application and persistence. Incentives for teamwork, as well as means to identify powerful joint proposals, etc. will have to be put in place. By informal contacts, as well as by forming teams of individuals best suited to address a specific project, the staff of the KTT office can be a positive force in moving away from such an insular mentality. They must be encouraged to pursue this actively.

Fostering the entrepreneurial spirit among students

Universities must inject more of an appreciation of the entrepreneurial attitude in their students. The latter must be encouraged to have a self-starting quality and to take more risks and initiatives. This can be done by including sessions on entrepreneurship, or using relevant examples in existing courses, as well as by inviting guest speakers presenting testimonials, thus acting as inspiring role models for the students.

Entrepreneurship is a natural companion of innovation. The energy and the passion of the entrepreneurs carry through the innovation and entrepreneurial spirit must be found in all corners of society, including, indeed, the public sector – not only in start-ups.

The role of universities in fostering more of an entrepreneurial spirit in students will only be pursued successfully if it is supported by society at large. The media, and entrepreneurs as role models, have a reinforcing impact in this area. Government policies must also be aligned: in France, the success of the new status of 'auto-entrepreneurs' (more than 250,000 in 2009) is impacting on public opinion. In the USA, the Senate is considering instituting a 'Start-up visa' lasting two years, to make it easier for entrepreneurs to come to the country. Singapore has a comprehensive set of actions to promote entrepreneurship. With regard to removing barriers, for example, Switzerland's punishing bankruptcy laws should be changed. Also, the bureaucratic and legal jungle in numerous countries must be streamlined.

Very importantly, the role of universities as a competent and *independent voice* is sorely needed in our often confused and impatient world. This independence must be carefully safeguarded by the statutes and the governance of the university, as discussed below.

Caveat: we need the independent voice of universities

In their drive to secure more deals with firms, universities must be careful not to become excessively greedy, loosing the balance with their fundamental roles in research and teaching. Also, they should not become too influenced by an external customer that would become dominant.

In our sometimes confused world, more than ever, we need universities to retain a precious role as independent voices. They should not be unduly influenced by a specific industry, firm or non-governmental organization. The researchers and the institution must keep their freedom and independence. We need them to inform the public debate.

The University of Berkeley offers a useful example in the way it has targeted its guidelines at avoiding the possibility of one actor excessively influencing any part of the university. The text of a 1998 document[4] first highlights that collaborations on a large scale present risks as well as benefits. The main risk is that it may distract the university from its teaching mission and public-interest research. This issue can be handled by employing transparent, faculty-led governance including clear criteria. The values of academic freedom, non-discrimination and intellectual property must be safeguarded, as well as the standard university practices regarding hiring personnel and grant-making processes.

Conclusion

With the Wall Street tsunami in 2008, hubris, herd behaviour, greed and taking the short-term view, far more than in the past, have greatly accelerated the ruin of most of the OECD economies and hastened a massive shift of power to Asia. Years ago, Philip Augar's *The Greedmerchants*[5] alerted us to some of the underlying causes of this financial pandemic. The rapidity and the brutality of the resulting crisis were more acute than in 1929 because they were exacerbated by globalization.

As the common wisdom says: 'do not waste a crisis'. This cataclysm must be taken as an opportunity to transform many elements of our 'system'. We should embrace a longer-term view, diligently work towards enhanced sustainability, and pay much more attention to Asia. This means that we need many innovations, as well as a less conformist – even a bold – attitude for positive change. With their fresh inputs 'from another world', universities and public laboratories must play their full part in this transformation.

As a reminder of the fact that, in this book, we have focused on one part of the mission of universities, let us look at a recent OECD study on tertiary education.[6] This study underscores the fact that tertiary education institutions fulfill several roles and it is important not to limit any analysis on the economic role alone. The economic functions of tertiary education, which take place through human resource development, R&D and knowledge and technology diffusion, are not the sole role of the system. Universities support many fields of knowledge that have no economic role to speak of, yet are of enormous social and cultural significance.

At the time of the breakthrough represented by the advent of synthetic life, announced by the media in May 2010, it is opportune to underline that this work was largely made possible by the publicly funded genome research. This remarkable breakthrough is presented by some as opening Pandora's box, out of which Frankenstein will jump. This landmark step is the precursor of many advances towards medical treatments, as well as providing various substitutes for current oil-based materials so fundamental to our existing societies.

In our internet world, it is also appropriate to underscore that a government-supported research laboratory, the particle physics institute, CERN, in Geneva, Switzerland, invented a key piece of the architecture of the world wide web.

In the complex process involved in going from science to business by transferring knowledge and technology from universities to firms for value-creation, there are three main elements:

- universities and public research laboratories, providing ideas, knowledge, expertise and different points of view;
- partnering firms, ready to look at new areas and novel approaches;
- the knowledge and technology transfer process linking the two.

Each of these elements must be well functioning and aligned to do the job of turning projects, including on non-technical issues, into value-creating activities. The framework conditions must support this process.

In terms of specific areas for the partnerships, high priority must be put on: (1) healthcare, where it is urgent, partly because of demographics, to innovate in order to provide good healthcare at relatively low cost; (2) ICTs, where we are only beginning to capture the potential of the enabling technologies for connections and distributions, new business models, creating true value for customers, as well as more efficient operations; (3) 'greener' technologies and practices, in order to move the world to a more sustainable state, while providing new opportunities. Growth must be more on value-adding than on quantitative consumption and the lifestyles of individuals must change; (4) IT security is not always a recognized priority, particularly in the financial services, where institutions have merged without understanding the implications for the security of the computer networks on which their data is kept. A big scandal is bound to erupt in this area, which will be a wake-up call for the sleep-walking managers. For some time, the military sector has taken cyber security seriously. It also sees the internet not only as a tool, but also a battlefield in electronic space.

The optimum situation for firms engaging with universities would combine the following characteristics from various countries:

- The pragmatic, no-nonsense, not too legalistic approach to business exhibited in Switzerland.
- The high quality of research ... and the effectiveness of its transfer, also in Switzerland.
- The high entrepreneurial spirit and 'can do' attitude shown in the USA and China.
- The policies for universities' excellence and sustained support of research in place in the UK – although, in the spring of 2010, there is talk of reducing, by £500 million, the amount of investment in science and education over the next few years.
- Singapore's relentless efforts to provide a positive, entrepreneurial environment to value-creation, resulting in being number one for competitiveness, according to the 2010 IMD Competitiveness Yearbook.

Whatever the country, governments must relentlessly focus on innovation-led growth and job-creation. They must do this much more intently than they currently do. One positive example is Singapore, which has been among the top five most competitive countries in recent years and made it to the top position in 2010. Competitiveness is all about providing an environment where investments and entrepreneurial initiatives prosper, creating jobs as a result. Singapore has a very low unemployment rate, while having a strong flow of immigrants.

Governments must have job-creation as an absolute priority. They must show leadership and resilience in providing the conditions to turn innovations into productive outcome. For this, they must remove existing barriers, put in place educational, legal and fiscal policies, simplify and streamline regulatory and legislative mazes, as well as developing infrastructures, in telecommunications and transport, which foster positive dynamics in this area.

As an integral part of this process, vibrant partnerships between firms and universities must play a much more effective role in the value-creation process, while moving our world towards a more sustainable state.

Notes

1 Firms engage with universities in many different ways

1. Georges Haour, *Resolving the Innovation Paradox: Enhancing Growth in Technology Companies*, London: Palgrave Macmillan, 2004. The website of the book is: http://www.innovationparadox.com.
2. *Lambert Review on Business–University Collaboration* (2003), http://www.hm-treasury.gov.uk.
3. Ibid., p. 24.
4. Gordon Binder, *Science Lessons*, Harvard: Harvard University Press, 2008, p. 22.
5. Alec Broers, *The Triumph of Technology*, Cambridge: Cambridge University Press, 2005.
6. Speech of R. Levin at the Royal Society, London, February 1, 2010, http://opa.yale.edu/president/message.aspx?id=91.
7. 'Unlocking Innovation in China', *Economist* Intelligence Report, 2009.
8. IMD Case Study on Infosys, 2008.
9. *Higher Ambitions: The Future of Universities in a Knowledge Economy*, report from the UK Department by Business, Innovation & Skills, 2009.

2 Collaborative research between companies and universities

1. See www.lambertreview.com.
2. *Responsible Partnering: A Guide to Better Practices for Collaborative Research between Science and Industry* (2005, updated in 2009). This document can be downloaded from the website of the European Industrial Research Management Association, headquartered in Paris (www.eirma.asso.fr).

3. *Metrics for the Evaluation of Knowledge Transfer Activities at Universities*, report commissioned by UNICO, university of Tokyo (2008). This report, which can be downloaded from www.library-house.net, has been prepared with the help of Professor Kevin Cullen, Head of Research Enterprise at the University of Glasgow.
4. *Guidelines for Companies Seeking Research Collaboration with Cornell University* (Cornell University, 2008).
5. See www.nationalacademies.org.

3 Firms accessing university technology through licenses

1. AUTM report for 2008, covering 191 US offices for knowledge and technology transfer; see www.autm.org.
2. Ibid.
3. Ibid.
4. K. Ku, 'Is Technology Transfer a Winning Proposition?', in B. J. Le Beouf, Robert C. Miller, and Associates, *Developing University–Industry Relations*, San Francisco: Jossey-Bass, 2009, pp. 17–30.
5. H. U. D. Wiesendanger, *Technology Licensing at Stanford University*, California: Stanford University, 1996.
6. See, for example, J. Bessen and M. J. Meurer, *Patent Failure*, Princeton, NJ: Princeton University Press, 2008.
7. J. Michael Finger and Philip Schuler, *Poor People's Knowledge: Promoting Intellectual Property in Developing Countries*, Oxford: Oxford University Press, 2004.
8. *Harvard Business Review*, March 2010, p. 40.
9. Bessen and Meurer, *Patent Failure*.
10. Finger and Schuler, *Poor People's Knowledge*.
11. J. Thursby, A. Fuller and M. Thursby, 'US Faculty Patenting: Inside and Outside the University', *Research Policy*, vol. 38, no. 1, 2009, pp. 1–25.
12. R. Geiger, *Tapping the Riches of Science*, Harvard: Harvard University Press, 2008.
13. Ibid., p. 131.
14. OECD Review, *China*, OECD, 2008, www.oecd.org.
15. Ibid.
16. See www.tubitak.gov.tr.

4 Firms accessing university research results via spin-outs

1. Georges Haour, 'Israel: A Powerhouse for Networked Entrepre-neurship', *Journal of Entrepreneurship and Innovation Management*, vol. 5, 2005, pp. 39–50.
2. Graham Richards, *Spin-Outs: Creating Businesses from University Intellectual Property*, Hampshire: Harriman, 2009.
3. *Investing in the Enterprise*, British Venture Capital Association report, Library House, 2006.
4. *Higher Ambitions: The Future of Universities in a Knowledge Economy,* report from the UK Department for Business, Innovation and Skills, 2009.
5. AUTM report for 2008; see www.autm.org.
6. IMD Case Study on Infosys, 2008.
7. Haour, 'Israel'.
8. R. J. Artley, G. Dobrauz, G. E. Plasoning, and R. R. Strasser, *Making Money Out of Technology: Best Practice in Technology Exploitation from Academic Sources*, Pennsylvania: Linde International, 2003.
9. Ibid.

5 SMEs must engage with universities

1. J. E. Stiglitz and S. J. Wallsten, 'Public–Private Technology Partner-ships: Promises and Pitfalls', *American Behavioral Scientist*, vol. 43, no. 1, 1999, pp.52–73.
2. C. W. Wessner, *Committee on Capitalizing on Science, Technology, and Innovation: An Assessment of the Small Business Innovation Research Program*, National Research Council, 2008.
3. Stiglitz and Wallsten, 'Public–Private Technology Partnerships'.
4. Report of the Hearing the US House of Representatives' Committee on Science and Technology, April 26, 2007.
5. *European Union Bulletin on the Small Business Act*, Summer 2008.
6. Sigvald Harryson, 'Flexibility in Innovation through External Learning: Exploring Models for Industry–University Collaboration', *Journal of Technology Management*, 2008.
7. Annual Report of the Finnish agency Tekes, 2008.

8. B. Hall, F. Lotti and J. Mairesse, *Innovation and Productivity in SMEs: Empirical Study for Italy*, 2009; see www.cide.info/conf/2009.
9. See www.businessgrowthinitiative.org.
10. *OECD Science, Technology and Industry Outlook*, 2008, p. 38.
11. *Partnerships for Innovation*, NSERC report, Ottawa, Canada, 2009.

6 Best practices for firm–university partnerships

1. European Innovation Scoreboard (2009).
2. Ibid.
3. Global Competitiveness Index (World Economic Forum, 2009–10).
4. IMD World Competitiveness Yearbook (2010).
5. A. Arundel and C. Bordoy, *The 2006 ASTP Survey*, The Hague: Association of European Science and Technology Transfer Professionals, 2006.
6. A. Conti and P. Gaulé, *The CEMI Survey of University Technology Transfer Offices in Europe*, working papers series, 2008.
7. Ibid.
8. D. A. King, 'The Scientific Impact of Nations', *Nature*, vol. 430, no. 6997, 2004, pp. 311–16.
9. Conti and Gaulé, *The CEMI Survey of University Technology Transfer Offices in Europe*.
10. H. U. D. Wiesendanger, *Technology Licensing at Stanford University*, California: Stanford University, 1996.
11. *Reviews on Innovation Policy: Switzerland*, Paris: OECD, 2006: 'the recent development of technology transfer offices (TTO) in universities is a welcome step, and their activities should be further expanded'.
12. Higher Education Innovation Fund 4; see www.hefce.ac.uk/econsoc/buscom/heif/.
13. *Reviews on Innovation Policy: Switzerland*, OECD.
14. See also a similar UK initiative from 2004–9; www.hefce.ac.uk/econsoc/buscom/heif/centres/.
15. www.researchnl.com/funding/rdvouchers.htm.

16. www.senternovem.nl/mmfiles/Subsidieregeling%20innovatievouc hers%202006%20in%20Staatscourant_tcm24-188082.pdf.
17. www.innovationvouchers.ie/.
18. M. Cornet, B. Vroomen et al., *Do Innovation Vouchers Help SMEs to Cross the Bridge Towards Science?*, CPB Netherlands Bureau for Economic Policy Analysis, 2006.
19. D. Guellec and B. V. P. De La Potterie, 'The Impact of Public R&D Expenditure on Business R&D', *Economics of Innovation and New Technology*, vol. 12, no. 3, 2003, pp. 225–43.

7 The way forward

1. *Knowledge for Growth*, report of the expert group at DG Research, 2007. See www.ec.europe.eu/investinresearch.
2. As reported in the silicon fen business report, March 18, 2009. See www.siliconfenbusiness.com.
3. *Knowledge for Growth*, DG Research.
4. See http://www.academic–senate.berkeley.edu on university–industry partnerships.
5. P. Augar, *The Greedmerchants*, Harmondsworth: Penguin, 2005.
6. *Tertiary Education for the Knowledge Society*, Paris: OECD, 2008.

Select Bibliography

Bessant John and Tim Venables (eds), *Creating Wealth from Knowledge: Meeting the Innovation Challenge*, Cheltenham: Elgar, 2008.

Binder, Gordon, *Science Lessons*, Harvard: Harvard University Press, 2008.

Blaize-Hazard, Catherine, *Les contrats d'exploitation des droits des brevets*, Paris: Tec & Doc, 2005.

Bok, Derek, *Universities in the Marketplace*, Princeton, NJ: University of Princeton Press, 2003.

Broers, Alec, *The Triumph of Technology*, Cambridge: Cambridge University Press, 2005.

Brunswold, Brian, *Drafting Patent License Agreements*, Washington DC: Bureau of National Affairs, 2004.

Emmott, Bill, *Rivals: How the Power Struggle between China, India and Japan will Shape our Next Decade*, Harmondsworth: Allen Lane/Penguin, 2008.

Finger, J. Michael and Philip Schuler (eds), *Poor People's Knowledge: Promoting Intellectual Property in Developing Countries*, Oxford: Oxford University Press, 2004.

Gao, Zhicun, *Technology Transfer in China's Industrial Development: Consequences, Policy and Reforms*, Saarbrücken: Lambert, 2010.

Geiger, Roger, *Tapping the Riches of Science*, Harvard: Harvard University Press, 2008.

Haour, Georges, *Resolving the Innovation Paradox: Enhancing Growth in Technology Companies*, London: Palgrave Macmillan, 2004.

Libermann, A. (ed.), *Licensing and Technology Transfer: Practice and the Law*, London: Kluwer, 2008.

LiHua, Richard, *Technology and Knowledge Transfer in China*, Surrey: Ashgate, 2003.

Mowery, David, *Ivory Tower and Industrial Revolution: university–Industry Technology Transfer Before and After the Bayh-Dole Act*, Stanford: Stanford University Press, 2004.

Nilekani, Nandan, *Imagining India*, Harmondsworth: Penguin, 2008.

Pisano, Gary, *Science Business: The Promise, the Reality and the Future of Biotech*, Harvard: Harvard Business School Press, 2006.

Razgaitis, Richard, *Valuation and Deal-making of Technology-based Intellectual Property*, Kindle, 2009.

Richards, Graham, *Spin-outs: Creating Businesses from University Intellectual Property*, Hampshire: Harriman, 2009.

Seifert, Ralf (ed.), *Nurturing Science-based Ventures*, New York: Springer, 2008.

Speser, Phyllis, *The Art and Science of Technology Transfer*, New York: Wiley, 2006.

Stolz, Cornelia, *Small Firms and Innovation Policy in Japan*, New York: Routledge, 2006.

Teece, David, *The Transfer and Licensing of Know How and Intellectual Property*, New Jersey: World Scientific, 2008.

Thanh Ngyen, Tu, *Competition Law, Technology Transfer and the TRIPS Agreement: Implications for Developing Countries*, Cheltenham: Elgar, 2010.

Weber, Luc and James Duderstadt (eds), *Reinventing the Research University*, Connecticut: Economica, 2004.

Weber, Luc and James Duderstadt (eds), *University Research for Innovation*, Connecticut: Economica, 2010.

Weiss, C. and W.Bonvillian, *Structuring an Energy Revolution*, Cambridge, MA: MIT Press, 2009.

Reports

Higher Ambitions: The Future of Universities in a Knowledge Economy, report from the UK Department for Business, Innovation and Skills, 2009.

Innovationactivitaten in der Schweiz, Bern: SECO, 2010.

Rapport sur la valorisation de la recherche, Rapport M 016 01 de l'Inspection Générale des Finances, French Ministry of Finance, January 2005.

Technology Transfer, Intellectual Property and Effective University–Industry Partnerships: Experiences of China, India, Japan, World Intellectual Property Organization, 2007; see www.wipo.int.

Periodicals

Electronic journal *Science/Business*; see info@sciencebusiness.net.

Les Nouvelles, publication from the Licensing Society.

Journal of Technology Management in China, Emerald; www.emeraldinsight.com/jtmc.htm.

Global news and best practices for managers of innovation and intellectual property; see www.beyondfirstworld.com.

Shanghai International Technology Transfer Network; see www.STTNet.

Index

Key: **bold** = extended discussion or term highlighted in the text; f = figure; n = note.

———————